GUS WÜSTEMANN

Der italienische Architekt und Architekturtheoretiker Aldo Rossi verglich die Architektur mit den Wissenschaften. Wie diese schreite die Architektur voran, indem sie stetig auf bereits Erreichtes aufbaue und sich so weiterentwickele. Diesem wissenschaftlichen Aspekt dient diese Buchreihe. Seit 2000 dokumentiert sie die aktuelle Schweizer Architektur. Die Reihe wird in ihrer Kontinuität gleichsam zu einem Gedächtnis der Architektur, das die Werke dem Vergessen entzieht. Von den mit hohem Qualitätsanspruch ausgewählten Architekturschaffenden werden die wichtigsten Bauten festgehalten, ausführlich dargestellt und dokumentiert. Jeder Band dient auch der Reflexion über den architektonischen Willen, der hinter den Projekten steht. So sind in dieser Reihe mehr oder minder alle in der Schweiz wirkenden Architekturkritikerinnen und Architekturkritiker mit einzelnen oder mehreren Textbeiträgen vertreten.

Der Hauptteil in jedem Band widmet sich dagegen der Welt der Anschauung. So sind jeweils anhand von Bildern und Plänen einige bemerkenswerte Bauten dargestellt, die nicht einer routinierten «Produktion» entsprungen sind. Vielmehr steht hinter jedem Entwurf eine leidenschaftliche Auseinandersetzung mit der Aufgabe und deren Prämissen.

Heinz Wirz
Verleger

The Italian architect and architectural theoretician Aldo Rossi compared architecture to the sciences. Like them, architecture progresses by constantly building upon what has already been achieved and develops further in this way. Since 2000, this series of books has been dedicated to the same academic approach in documenting contemporary Swiss architecture. It therefore becomes a form of architectural memory, ensuring that the architecture is not forgotten. The most important buildings by each of the selected high-quality architects are presented, described in detail and documented. Each volume also serves to reflect upon the architectural motivation behind the projects. By now, more or less every architectural critic working in Switzerland has contributed one or more articles to the series.

However, the core of each book is dedicated to the world of observation. Images and plans present a number of remarkable buildings that are not the result of routine "production". Instead, each design stems from a passionate engagement with the task and its premises.

Heinz Wirz
Publisher

GUS WÜSTEMANN

+ Team

QUART

Niemals werde ich jenen Tag vergessen, den ich mit Gus Wüstemann in Zürich verbrachte. Ich hatte bereits sein aussergewöhnliches Zuhause Crusch Alba in Barcelona gesehen und war mir daher seiner Fähigkeit bewusst, alles Vorgefundene – egal wie rau oder widerspenstig – in etwas Schönes zu verwandeln. Und mir war klar, dass er ein Händchen dafür hat, neue Architektur in alte Gebäude zu integrieren, ohne die Reinheit von einem der beiden zu opfern. (Die elegante Küche und das Badezimmer der Wohnung schienen nicht gebaut worden zu sein, sondern sich im Science-Fiction-Stil in einem 100-jährigen gotischen Gebäude materialisiert zu haben). Die gegebenen Bedingungen waren Gus' Inspiration, nicht sein Fluch.

Ich hatte auch schon viele Fotos von seinen Bauten gesehen und wusste, dass er Gebäude aus Betonplatten zu errichten vermag, die keine Zugeständnisse an die Dinge des Alltags zu machen scheinen. (Wo in den massiven Blöcken, die Gus als Wände, Böden und Decken verwendet, befinden sich die Rohre? Die Lichtschalter? Die Lüftungsschächte?) Bauten wie sein Apartmenthaus Stone H erscheinen ebenso geologisch wie architektonisch. Naturgewalten, die sich nicht von trivialen Dingen bremsen lassen.

Mir war klar, dass er diese Objekte im Auftrag einer wohlhabenden Bauherrschaft erstellt, die ein Vermögen für Glaswände ausgeben kann, die in dezenten Laibungen verschwinden, oder für Küchengeräte, die in ihrem Minimalismus Gus' Wunsch gerecht werden, vollständig unsichtbar zu sein. An jenem Tag in Zürich war ich also begeistert, wenn auch nicht sonderlich überrascht von seinem Haus Z22, in dem, wie er sagt, keine minderwertigen Materialien vorzufinden sind; und vom Projekt 2 Verandas, bei dem die Grenze zwischen innen und aussen nicht greifbar ist. Nachdem wir diese beiden Bauten besichtigt hatten, wollte er, dass ich mir sein Projekt für erschwinglichen Wohnraum an der Langgrütstrasse ansehe. Ich zögerte: Es war spät, ich war müde, und wann hatte zuletzt jemand Wohnraum in diesem Segment gebaut, der eine Fahrt durch die Stadt im Berufsverkehr gerechtfertigt hätte?

Ich hätte Gus nicht unterschätzen sollen. Was ich an der Langgrütstrasse sah, war möglicherweise der reinste Ausdruck seiner Philosophie – trotz geringem Budget. (Oder vielleicht gerade deshalb.) Gus' Gebäude ist im Wesentlichen ein Betonblock, in den zwei breite vertikale Schlitze gemeisselt worden sind. Die Wohnräume scheinen in diesen Schlitzen zu schweben, auf Bodenplatten, die eher wie fliegende Teppiche erscheinen. Die Räume sind so herausragend in ihren Details (sprich: undetailliert) wie bei all seine Wohnbauten im unerschwinglichen Segment. Das Inventar ist auf ein Minimum reduziert und die Materialpalette ist, gelinde gesagt, begrenzt. Die Schönheit des Raums erwächst aus seinen kraftvollen Formen, seiner Beziehung zur Sonne und seiner Schlichtheit. Ich wollte direkt einziehen, doch es war Zeit, in mein (ganz und gar konventionelles) Hotel zurückzukehren. Dort träumte ich von einer kompromisslosen Architektur.

Fred A. Bernstein

I will never forget the day I spent with Gus Wüstemann in Zurich. I had already been to his astonishing home, Crusch Alba, in Barcelona, so I was aware of his ability to transform whatever he found, no matter how rough or unruly, into something beautiful. And I knew he had a knack for inserting new architecture into old buildings without sacrificing the purity of either. (The apartment's sleek kitchen and bathroom seemed not to have been built but rather to have materialised, sci-fi style, inside a 100-year-old Gothic building.) Existing conditions were Gus's inspiration, not his bane.

I had also seen many photos of his work, so I knew that he had a gift for creating buildings out of slabs of concrete that seemed to make no concessions to quotidian matters. (Where, in the solid blocks that Gus uses as walls, floors and ceilings, are the pipes? The light switches? The vents?) Buildings like his Apartment House Stone H seemed as geological as they were architectural. Forces of nature, not held back by trivial concerns.

I knew he did these things for wealthy clients, who could spend a fortune for glass walls that vanish into discrete pockets, or for kitchen appliances sufficiently minimalist to satisfy Gus's wish that they disappear entirely. So on that day in Zurich, I was delighted, though not especially surprised, by his House Z22, where, as he says, there are no inferior materials and 2 Verandas, where the dividing line between indoors and outdoors is imperceptible. After we had visited those projects, he wanted me to see his affordable housing at Langgrütstrasse. I was reluctant to make the trip. It was late, I was tired and when was the last time anyone made affordable housing worth a drive across town in rush-hour traffic?

I should not have underestimated Gus. What I saw at Langgrütstrasse was possibly the purest expression of his philosophy to date, despite having been built on a budget (or perhaps because of that budget). Gus's building was essentially a concrete boulder with two wide vertical slots carved into it. Living spaces seem to float in those slots, on floor plates that feel more like flying carpets. The spaces are as exquisitely detailed (read: undetailed) as any of his unaffordable housing. Fixtures are kept to a minimum and the material palette, to put it mildly, is limited. The beauty is in the powerful spatial forms, their relationship to the sun and their simplicity. I wanted to move in, but it was time to drive back to my (utterly conventional) hotel. There I dreamt of architecture without compromises.

Fred A. Bernstein

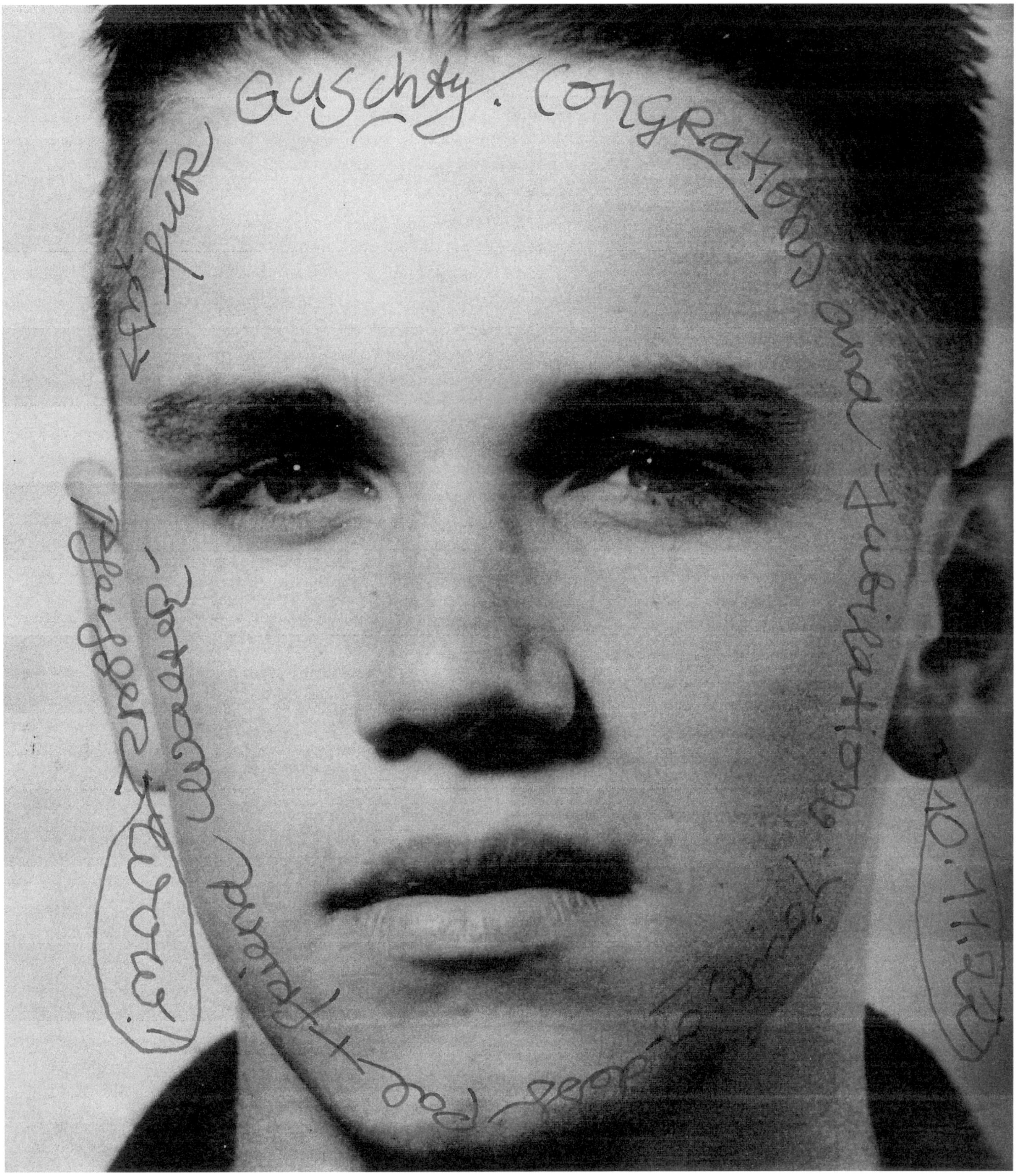

Walter Pfeiffer, 1984

UMBAU MEHRFAMILIENHAUS Z22 UND F88, ZÜRICH

HOUSE Z22 AND WAREHOUSE F88, ZURICH

Das Ensemble des Mehrfamilienhauses Z22 und F88 setzte sich vor dem Umbau aus einem niedrigen Gewerbetrakt und einem mehrgeschossigen spätklassizistischen Wohnhaus zusammen. Heute beherbergt es diverse Wohnungen und eine Galerie. Da im Innern kaum noch qualitätsvolle Bausubstanz existierte, wurde das historische Gemäuer in einem fast schon archäologischen Akt von späteren Schichten befreit, sodass nur noch die Primärstruktur erhalten blieb. Daraus resultierte ein «neuer alter» Zustand, den es in dieser Art nie gab. Unverputzte Steinmauern und unbehandeltes Holz treten in einen spielerischen Dialog mit industriellen Werkstoffen. Die Materialien sind nicht hierarchisch eingesetzt, die Dichotomie zwischen *high* und *low* wurde negiert und alte und neue Elemente wurden miteinander collagiert. Aus der Reibung von Beton und Holz, OSB-Platten und Polycarbonat entfaltet sich eine enorme Kraft. Vermeintliche Improvisation verbindet sich mit der Dauerhaftigkeit der Geschichte. Im Zusammenspiel mit den vorhandenen Fragmenten, die in den rustikalen Einbauten eine Fortsetzung finden, regen die kontrastierenden Werkstoffe die Fantasie an und erzeugen eine archaische Raumatmosphäre, die an Krypten, Ruinen oder Thermen erinnert. Gleichzeitig vermitteln die multifunktionalen Räume in ihrer sinnlichen Schlichtheit bescheidenen Luxus.

Before its conversion, the ensemble of the Z22 and F88 apartment building consisted of a low-rise commercial wing and a multi-storey late-Neoclassicist residential volume. Today, it accommodates various apartments and a gallery. Since there was hardly any quality in the interior building fabric, the later layers were removed from the historical walls in an almost archaeological measure, so that only the primary structure remained. The result is a "new old" condition that has never existed in that form before. Unplastered stone walls and untreated wood enter into a playful dialogue with the industrial materials. These are not used hierarchically, as the dichotomy of *high* and *low* was negated by collaging the old and new elements. The friction between concrete and wood, as well as OSB boards and polycarbonate, unleashes enormous power. Apparent improvisation connects with the endurance of history. In their interaction with existing fragments, which are picked up on with rustic fittings, the contrasting building materials inspire the imagination and create an archaic spatial atmosphere, resembling a crypt, ruin or spa. At the same time, the multifunctional rooms' sensorial simplicity expresses modest luxury.

Direktauftrag
Ausführung: 2015–2017
Bauherrschaft: Privat
Bauingenieur: Born Partner AG
Heizung, Lüftung, Kühlung und Sanitär: Frei+Partner Haustechnikplanung AG
Bauphysik: Gartenmann Engineering AG
Mitarbeit: Manuel Greter, Bianca Kilian, Valentin Kokudev, Daniel Pelach, Panagiota Sarantinoudi

Direct contract
Construction: 2015–2017
Client: Private
Civil engineer: Born Partner AG
Heating, ventilation, air conditioning and plumbing: Frei+Partner Haustechnikplanung AG
Building physics: Gartenmann Engineering AG
Team: Manuel Greter, Bianca Kilian, Valentin Kokudev, Daniel Pelach, Panagiota Sarantinoudi

5 m

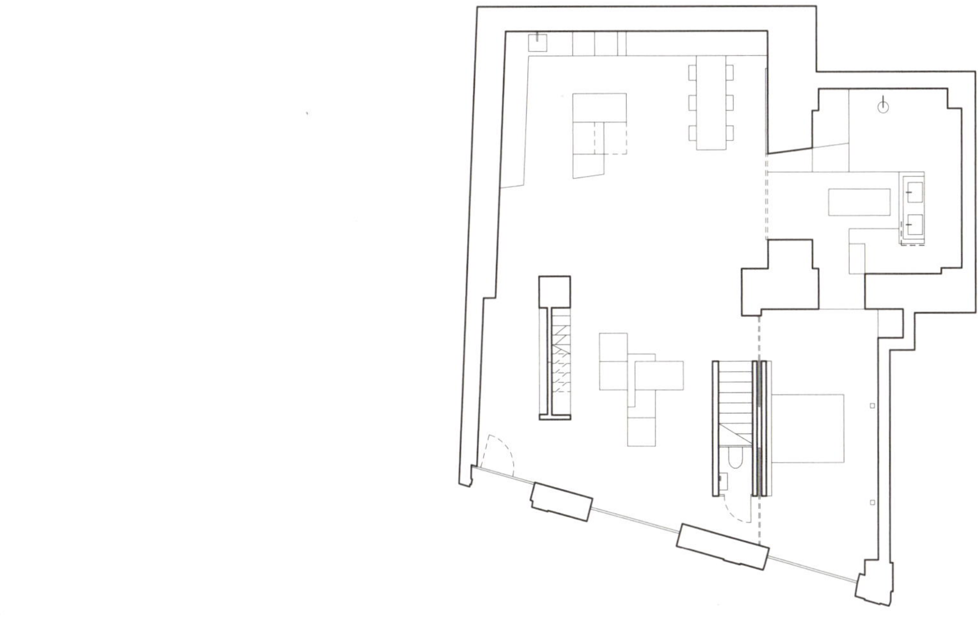
5m
N

MEHRFAMILIENHAUS STONE H, ZÜRICH

Die geometrisch simpel gehaltene Grundfigur basiert auf dem Buchstaben H. Entsprechend prägnant ist auch das architektonische Erscheinungsbild des durchmischten Wohnhauses Stone H, das eine hervorragende Aussicht, optimale Belichtung und ein hohes Mass an Privatsphäre bietet. Innen und Aussen sind in einer Art Raumkontinuum miteinander verbunden. Programmatisch besetzte Bereiche wie Badezimmer und Küche sind peripher angeordnet, wodurch ein offenes Wohnkonzept entsteht. Die teils kaschierten Elemente sind mitunter frei entfaltbar, die Mieterschaft kann sich individuell entfalten und ihre eigenen Ideen ausleben. Nicht eine konventionelle Fassade trennt das Innere vom Aussenraum, sondern flexibel verstellbare Schiebefenster. Dadurch interagiert die Architektur mit der Natur, denn sowohl der gedeckte Aussenraum als auch der Patio lassen sich unterschiedlich bespielen. Inspiriert durch Ruinen, entzieht sich das kraftvoll anmutende Wohnhaus den konformistisch-normativen Lebensschemata, indem es auf eine klassische, vordefinierte Raumeinteilung verzichtet. Die äussere Schicht der zweischaligen Betonstruktur wurde mit OSB-Platten gegossen und weist eine raue Oberfläche auf, während die innere einen glatten Charakter hat. In den Beton eingelassene Leuchten sorgen für indirektes Licht und eine besondere Atmosphäre.

STONE H APARTMENT BUILDING, ZURICH

The geometrically simple ground figure is based on the letter H. The architectural appearance of the Stone H apartment building is accordingly succinct, offering exceptional views, ideal lighting and a high degree of privacy. The interior and exterior are connected in a kind of spatial continuum. Programme-related areas such as the bathroom and kitchen are arranged peripherally, creating an open living concept. Some of the partially hidden elements can be developed individually and live out their own ideas. Instead of having one conventional façade to separate the interior and exterior, flexibly moveable sliding windows are used. In this way, the architecture interacts with the countryside, since both the covered exterior space and the patio can be occupied in different ways. Inspired by ruins, the mighty-looking residential building distances itself from conforming, normative lifestyles by doing without a classic, predefined spatial organisation. The outer layer of the concrete double-envelope was cast with OSB boards and has a coarse surface, while the inner side has a smooth character. Lights sunken into the concrete ensure indirect illumination and a special atmosphere.

Direktauftrag
Ausführung: 2011–2014
Bauherrschaft: Privat
Bauingenieur: Born Partner AG
Heizung, Lüftung, Kühlung und Sanitär: Frei+Partner Haustechnikplanung AG
Projektleiterin: Marta Balsera Goni
Mitarbeit: Jan Kubasiewicz, Eftychia Pathanasiou, Silvia Pujalte

Direct contract
Construction: 2011–2014
Client: Private
Civil engineer: Born Partner AG
Heating, ventilation, air conditioning and plumbing: Frei+Partner Haustechnikplanung AG
Project manager: Marta Balsera Goni
Team: Jan Kubasiewicz, Eftychia Pathanasiou, Silvia Pujalte

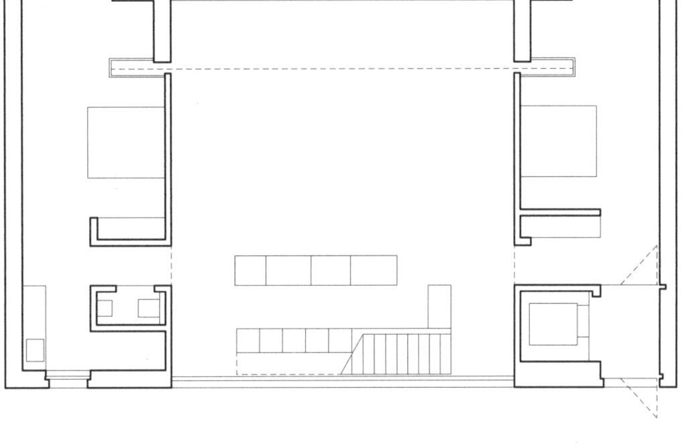

5m —— N

72
72

Die Erweiterung des Wien Museums am Karlsplatz reagiert auf die bestehende städtebauliche Situation, indem sie mit ihr in einen gestalterischen Dialog tritt. Der sogenannte Haerdtl-Bau aus den 1950er Jahren steht unter Denkmalschutz. Er musste saniert und in das Projekt integriert werden. Nach oben hin sind bündig zur alten Fassade mehrere Steinquader aufgesetzt. Sie entfalten eine markante, archaisch anmutende Präsenz, ohne den Massstab der benachbarten Bebauung, insbesondere der barocken Karlskirche, zu brechen. Kontrastierend zum Bestand ist die Oberflächenstruktur roher gehalten, und ebenso distanzieren sich die strassenseitig geschlossenen und kompakt ausgebildeten Volumen von der differenzierten Fassadengliederung des Haerdtl-Komplexes. In diesem sollen infolge der vielen Fenster nur noch Nutzungen mit Tageslicht stattfinden. Die neuen Museumbereiche im Unter- und im abschliessenden Obergeschoss sind morphologische Raumerweiterungen der bestehenden Anlage, aber ganz ohne Fenster. Sie weisen ausschliesslich Einschnitte auf, über welche bei Bedarf Tageslicht in die Ausstellungsräume gelangt. Das Erdgeschoss ist nun über eine grosse, massive Treppenlandschaft mit dem Untergeschoss verbunden und generiert so ein doppelgeschossiges Foyer. Die Erschliessung erfolgt über den Altbau.

The extension to the Wien Museum on Karlsplatz reacts to the existing urban-planning situation by entering into a design dialogue with it. The so-called Haerdtl Building from the 1950s is preservation-listed. It had to be renovated and integrated into the project. Several stone blocks have been placed higher up, flush with the old façade. They achieve a striking presence with an archaic appearance, without exceeding the scale of the neighbouring buildings, especially the Baroque Karlskirche. However, the surface structure is kept rawer than the existing buildings, while the volumes are closed and compact on the street side, distancing themselves from the differentiated façades of the Haerdtl complex. The latter will exclusively accommodate naturally lit uses due to its many windows. The new museum areas in the basement and adjoining upper level are morphological spatial extensions to the existing facility, albeit completely without windows. They merely have incisions to allow natural light to enter the exhibition rooms if required. The ground floor is now a large, massive staircase landscape connected to the basement, thereby creating a double-storey foyer. Access is provided via the old building.

Offener Wettbewerb: 2015, Finalist
Bauherrschaft: Wien Museum Neu
In Zusammenarbeit mit:
Frank + Partners Architektur
Bauingenieur: Schnetzer Puskas Ingenieure AG
Landschaftsarchitektur: Valentina Geselin
Heizung, Lüftung, Kühlung und Sanitär: Frei+Partner Haustechnikplanung AG
Bauphysik: Gartenmann Engineering AG
Mitarbeit: Valentin Kukodev, Daniel Pelach, Panagiota Sarantinoudi

Open competition: 2015, Finalist
Client: Wien Museum Neu
In collaboration with:
Frank+ Partners Architektur
Civil engineer: Schnetzer Puskas Ingenieure AG
Landscape architecture: Valentina Geselin
Heating, ventilation, air conditioning and plumbing: Frei+Partner Haustechnikplanung AG
Building physics: Gartenmann Engineering AG
Team: Valentin Kukodev, Daniel Pelach, Panagiota Sarantinoudi

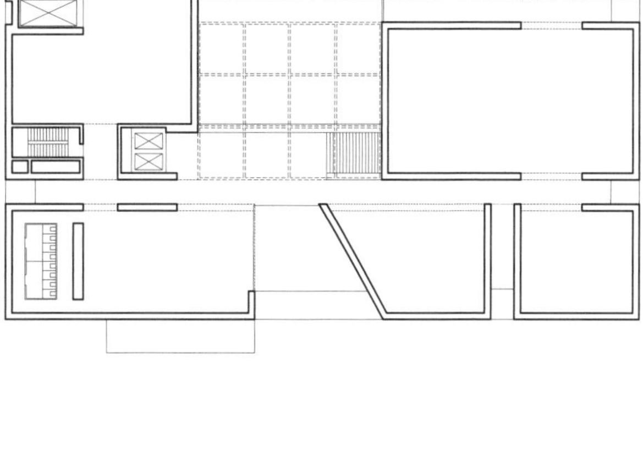

20 m Z

In prominenter Nachbarschaft zu Ludwig Mies van der Rohes Neuer Nationalgalerie und Hans Scharouns Berliner Philharmonie setzt der monolithische Komplex mit rauer Betontextur einen eigenen Akzent. Damit reiht er sich in die individualistische Bebauung des Kulturforums ein, die von unterschiedlichen Architektursprachen lebt. Der Solitär mit quadratischem Grundriss entfaltet eine introvertierte Geste, seine Fassaden sind platzseitig mehrheitlich geschlossen. So wird ein Kontrast zum ikonischen Museumsgebäude von Mies – jenem offenen Glas-Stahl-Kubus geradezu – erzeugt. Doch beide Bauten präsentieren sich als kompakte Volumen. Schliesslich interagiert der neue Museumsbau, der an der einen Ecke grosszügig eingeschnitten ist, auch mit der organisch entworfenen Philharmonie: Die dezent abgerundeten Eingangsbereiche korrespondieren mit der dynamischen Verspieltheit der Scharoun'schen Konzerthalle. Gleichzeitig verschmilzt der asketisch und zeitlos wirkende Kulturkomplex mit der Umgebung, denn an allen vier Ecken durchqueren grosse Passagen den vermeintlich isolierten Baukörper. Diese städtebauliche Einbindung greift den Geist der pulsierenden Metropole auf und leitet diesen als Raumkontinuum durch ein als offener Raum verstandenes Museum.

In the prominent vicinity of Ludwig Mies van der Rohe's Neue Nationalgalerie and Hans Scharoun's Berliner Philharmonie, the monolithic complex with a coarse concrete texture presents its own features. It thereby joins the other individualistic buildings at the Kulturforum, which thrives on differing architectural languages. The solitary building with a square floor-plan expresses an introverted gesture, while its façades facing the square are mostly closed. This creates a contrast to the iconic museum building by Mies, its open glass and steel cube achieving almost the opposite effect. However, both buildings present themselves as compact volumes. The new museum building, which is generously incised at one corner, also interacts with the organic design of the Philharmonie: the subtly rounded entrance areas correspond with the dynamic playfulness of the concert hall by Scharoun. At the same time, the ascetic and timeless appearance of the cultural complex merges with its surroundings, as large passages from all four corners cross the apparently isolated buildings. The urban-planning integration picks up on the spirit of the vibrant metropolis and applies it as a spatial continuum through the museum, which is grasped as an open space.

Offener Wettbewerb: 2016
Bauherrschaft: Stiftung Preussischer Kulturbesitz
Landschaftsarchitektur: LAbA Landscape Architecture by Almeida
Mitarbeit: Valentin Kokudev, Panagiota Sarantinoudi, Andrea Buchmeier

Open competition: 2016
Client: Stiftung Preussischer Kulturbesitz
Landscape architecture: LAbA Landscape Architecture by Almeida
Team: Valentin Kokudev, Panagiota Sarantinoudi, Andrea Buchmeier

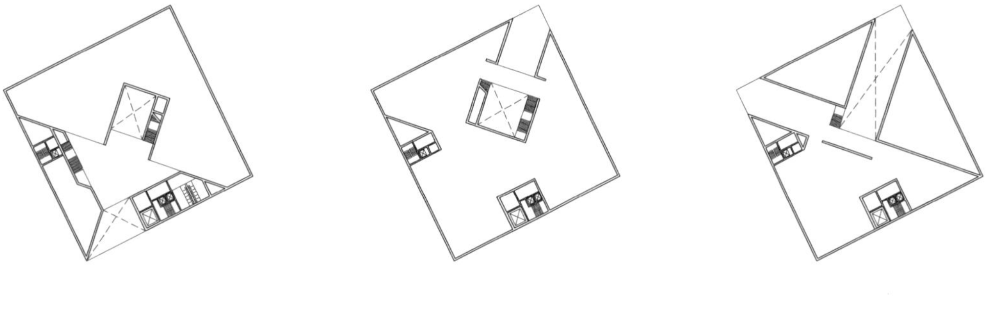

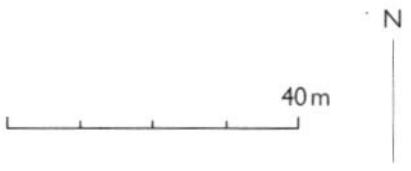
N
40 m

CAN BOSC I PLATJA, SANTANYÍ

Die Can Bosc i Platja im mallorquinischen Cala Llombards ist ein Strandhaus, das sich inmitten einer waldnahen Umgebung erhebt. Die simple, aber markante Betonstruktur zeichnet sich durch mehrere Diagonalen und versetzte Terrassen aus. Mit ihrem schlichten und teils auch transparent anmutenden Volumen fügt sie sich elegant in die topografische Situation am Hang. Dank seiner reduzierten Materialisierung mutet das Wohnhaus sehr ausdrucksstark an. Die einfache und ressourceneffiziente Ästhetik thematisiert zugleich ethische Fragen: Unkaschierte Materialien und die klare Struktur dominieren programmatische Aspekte; der Flexibilitätsanspruch verbindet sich mit einer Schichtung von Funktionen; die Einbauten beschränken sich auf ein absolutes Minimum. Das Ineinandergreifen von Innen und Aussen sowie unterschiedlich nutzbare, nicht normierte Bereiche charakterisieren diese Architektur, die ein hohes Mass an individueller Aneignung ermöglicht. Ein konstitutives Element bildet die Interaktion mit der Natur, sind doch die fliessend und offen entworfenen Innenräume durch die grossen Fenster ausgesprochen hell gehalten. Diverse Betontopografien bereichern die terrassierte Finca. Einer Oase gleich überführt sie das mediterrane Flair des Kontextes souverän in eine architektonische Form.

Can Bosc i Platja in the Majorcan town of Cala Llombards is a beach house that rises above its surroundings near a forest. The simple, but striking concrete structure is characterised by several diagonal, offset terraces. The simple, at times transparent-looking volume is elegantly integrated into the sloping topographical situation. The residential building's reduced materialisation gives it a very powerful expression, while the simple, resource-efficient aesthetics also engage with ethical considerations: unconcealed materials and the clear structure dominate programmatic aspects; the demand for flexibility is combined with a layering of functions; the fittings are limited to an absolute minimum. The dovetailed interior and exterior, as well as diversely usable, non-standard areas, characterise the architecture, which enables a high degree of individual appropriation. One constitutive element is formed by the interaction with the natural environment, since large windows ensure that the fluent, open interior spaces are kept extremely bright. Diverse concrete topographies enhance the terraced finca. Like an oasis, the building confidently translates the Mediterranean flair of the context into an architectural form.

Direktauftrag
Ausführung: 2022–2024
Bauherrschaft: Privat
Bauingenieur: BAC Engineering Consultancy Group
Heizung, Lüftung, Kühlung und Sanitär: amm Technical Group
Projektleiterin: Nerea Aranzabal
Mitarbeit: Bianca Kilian, Panagiota Sarantinoudi

Direct contract
Construction: 2022–2024
Client: Private
Civil engineer: BAC Engineering Consultancy Group
Heating, ventilation, air conditioning and plumbing: amm Technical Group
Project manager: Nerea Aranzabal
Team: Bianca Kilian, Panagiota Sarantinoudi

QUART
HIGHLIGHTS
2023/4
www.quart.ch

LANDHAUS VILLA AUMALLIA, FELANITX

Die Villa Aumallia, ein Landhaus in der Nähe von Felanitx auf Mallorca, verbindet traditionelle mallorquinische mit moderner Architektur. Die sorgfältige Auswahl lokaler Baumaterialien wie Mares-Stein und Holz für das Dach verankert das Gebäude organisch in seiner Umgebung.

Architektonisch besticht das Landhaus durch eine kontrollierte Struktur, die auf einem erhöhten Sockel über der Landschaft thront. Der u-förmige Grundriss mit einem grünen Innenhof als Mittelpunkt verweist auf historische Einflüsse aus der maurischen Architektur und fungiert als sozialer Knotenpunkt des Anwesens. Nachhaltigkeit ist ein zentrales Anliegen der Bauherrschaft, was sich im Einsatz erneuerbarer Energiequellen niederschlägt.

Die Villa Aumallia repräsentiert eine Verschmelzung von Geschichte und Moderne und bewahrt die kulturelle Identität Mallorcas, ohne dabei zeitgenössische Anforderungen an Nachhaltigkeit und Effizienz ausser Acht zu lassen. Sie steht für die gelungene Integration von modernen Werten in das traditionelle Erbe der lokalen Architektur.

VILLA AUMALLIA COUNTRY HOUSE, FELANITX

Villa Aumallia, a country house near Felanitx, Majorca, combines traditional Majorcan and modern architecture. The careful selection of local building materials, such as Marès stone and wood for the roof, anchors the building in its environment.

Architecturally, the country house impresses with its controlled structure, enthroned on an elevated plinth overlooking the landscape. The U-shaped ground plan, with a green inner courtyard, refers to historical influences of Moorish architecture and serves as the residence's social hub. Sustainability is a key concern for the client, as reflected in the use of renewable energy resources.

Villa Aumallia represents the merging of history and modernity, maintaining the cultural identity of Majorca, without ignoring contemporary requirements of sustainability and efficiency. It stands for the successful integration of modern values into the traditional heritage of the local architecture.

Direktauftrag
Ausführung: 2024–2026
Bauherrschaft: Privat
Mitarbeit: Nerea Aranzabal, Panagiota Sarantinoudi

Direct contract
Construction: 2024–2026
Client: Private
Team: Nerea Aranzabal, Panagiota Sarantinoudi

NEUER FORSCHUNGSCAMPUS FÜR DIE CHERNOVETSKY-STIFTUNG, KIEW

NEW RESEARCH CAMPUS FOR THE CHERNOVETSKY FOUNDATION, KIEV

Der neue Forschungscampus der Chernovetsky-Stiftung befindet sich auf einer langrechteckigen Parzelle inmitten einer stark begrünten Flusslandschaft. Seitlich rahmen mehrere Gebäude das grosse Areal, wodurch ein offener Platz entsteht, der die einzelnen Bauten durch präszise angelegte Wege und teils auch durch Sichtachsen miteinander verbindet. Das raumschiffartige Hauptzentrum ist als markanter zweigeschossiger Komplex mit abgeschrägten Ecken und zurückversetztem Eingangsbereich entworfen. Der Innenhof ist trapezförmig und nimmt die kantige Komposition des Betonkörpers auf. Materiell als auch formal kontrastiert er die anderen Pavillons des Ensembles: Die an den Längsseiten platzierten Häuser sind als transparente Glasstrukturen mit unterschiedlich geneigten Dachflächen gestaltet; die Anlage am Fluss setzt sich aus mehreren Dreiecken zusammen, von denen drei zum Wasser orientiert und komplett verglast sind. Neben einigen eher konventionell gehaltenen Büros sind die meisten Räume offen und zur freien, individuellen Aneignung angelegt. Die unterschiedlichen Geometrien und Formen sind für sich stets einfach zu erfassen und weisen jeweils eine eindeutige sowie schlichte Materialisierung auf. In ihrer diversen Gesamtheit verleihen sie dem architektonischen Ensemble aber einen repräsentativen und innovativen Charakter.

The new research campus of the Chernovetsky Foundation is situated on an elongated plot in the midst of a river landscape with lush vegetation. Several buildings frame the sides of the large grounds, creating an open square that connects the individual edifices by means of precisely placed walkways and a number of visual axes. The spaceship-like main centre is designed as a striking two-storey complex with oblique corners and a recessed entrance area. The interior courtyard has a trapezoid shape and picks up on the angular composition of the concrete volume. Both materially and formally, it contrasts with the ensemble's other pavilions: the buildings placed on the longitudinal sides are designed as transparent glass structures with differently slanting roofs; the facility by the river consists of several triangles, three of which are orientated towards the water and are fully glazed. In addition to a number of more conventional offices, most spaces are open and conceived for free, individual appropriation. The varying geometries and forms are easily grasped in themselves and each have a clear, simple materialisation. However, in their diverse unity, they give the architectural ensemble a prestigious, innovative character.

Eingeladener Wettbewerb: 2019, 2. Preis
Bauherrschaft: Chernovetsky-Stiftung
Bauingenieur: Dr. Schwartz Consulting AG
Mitarbeit: Bianca Kilian, Panagiota Sarantinoudi, Andre Sashko

Invited competition: 2019, 2nd Prize
Client: Chernovetsky Foundation
Civil engineer: Dr. Schwartz Consulting AG
Team: Bianca Kilian, Panagiota Sarantinoudi, Andre Sashko

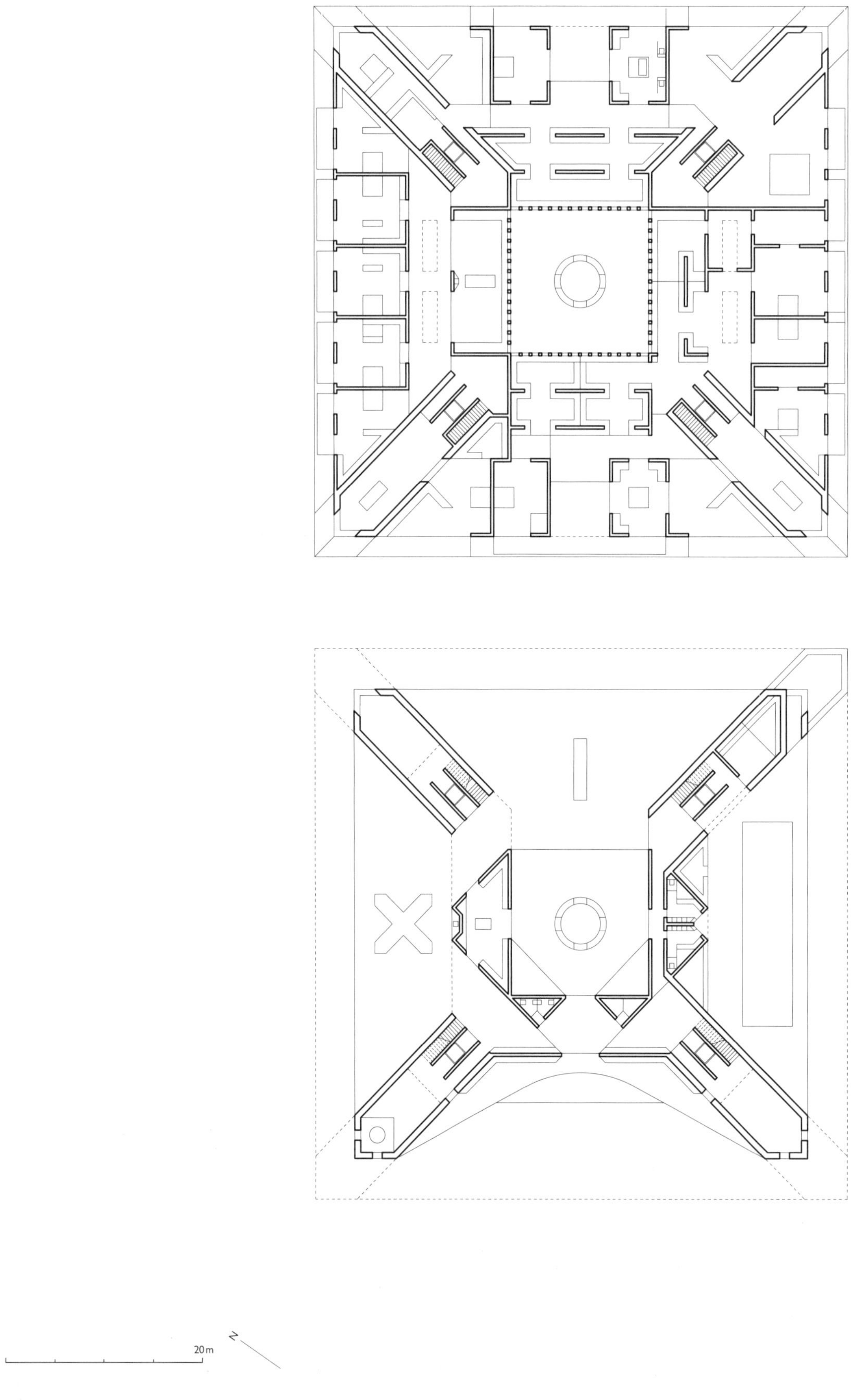
20 m
N

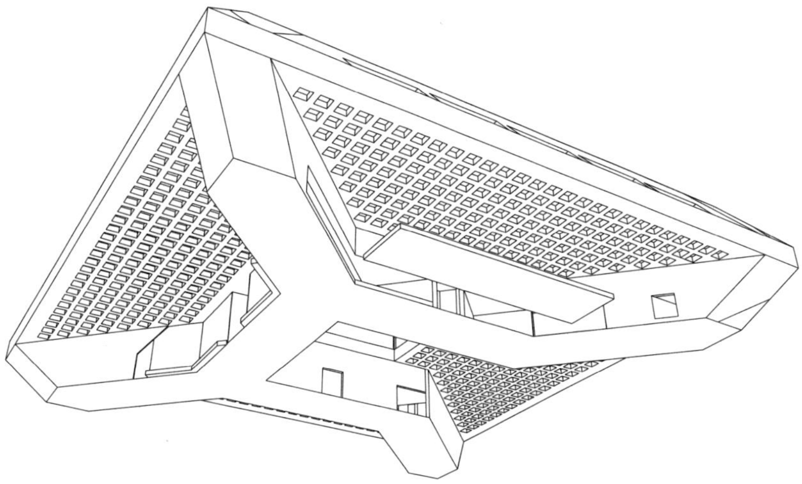

BEZAHLBARER WOHNRAUM FÜR ALLE, LANGGRÜTSTRASSE, ZÜRICH

Der markante, aber dennoch unaufdringlich gestaltete Solitär in der Langgrütstrasse im durchgrünten Stadtkörper von Zürich-Albisrieden bietet bezahlbaren Wohnraum für alle. Er kontrastiert die rechtwinklig zueinander angeordneten Zeilenbauten aus den 1950er Jahren. Der mitunter aus rohem Recyclingbeton gefertigte Monolith entstand im Auftrag der Baechi Stiftung und umfasst neun Wohnungen im fairen Mietsegment. Ressourceneffizienz ist auf mehreren Ebenen ein relevantes Thema. Einfache Materialien bestimmen das Erscheinungsbild, alle Einbauten sind auf ein absolutes Minimum reduziert und der Flexibilitätsanspruch ist mit einer Schichtung von Funktionen verbunden. So lässt sich der Küchentisch ausziehen oder der Herd verdecken, um die Ablage anderweitig nutzen zu können. Durch verschiedene Nutzungsoptionen ergeben sich vielfältige Raummomente. Simpel sind auch die Grundrisse: Die Räume sind fliessend konzipiert; die Schiebetüren trennen die einzelnen Bereiche nie komplett, da sie den Boden nicht berühren. Ein besonderes Merkmal sind die ausgeschnittenen Patios. Sie dienen nicht nur als Wohn- und Aussenräume, sondern durch ihre West-Ost-Ausrichtung auch als Sonnenbrücken. Diese Elemente verbinden die Architektur mit der Natur und sorgen für ein mediterranes Feeling – insbesondere im Sommer, wenn eine frische Brise durch den Patio weht.

AFFORDABLE HOUSING FOR ALL, LANGGRÜTSTRASSE, ZURICH

The prominent, yet unobtrusively designed free-standing building in Langgrütstrasse, in the green urban neighbourhood of Zurich-Albisrieden, provides affordable housing for all. It contrasts with the perpendicularly arranged housing rows of the 1950s. The monolith, which is partially made of raw, recycled concrete, was commissioned by the Baechi Foundation and comprises nine apartments in a fair rent-price segment. Resource-efficiency is a relevant theme on several levels. Simple materials determine the building's appearance, while all fittings are reduced to an absolute minimum and flexibility demands are combined with the layering of functions. In this way, a kitchen table can be pulled out and the cooker can be covered to use the surface differently. Various use options provide the potential for diverse spatial moments. The floor plans are also simple: the rooms are conceived fluently, while the sliding doors never partition the individual areas completely, since they do not touch the floor. One special feature is the excavated patios. They not only serve as living and exterior spaces, but also as sun bridges through their east-west orientation. These elements connect the architecture to the surrounding environment and ensure a Mediterranean atmosphere – especially in the summer, when a fresh breeze wafts over the patio.

Direktauftrag
Ausführung: 2017–2019
Bauherrschaft: I+B Baechi Stiftung
Bauingenieur: Born Partner AG
Heizung, Lüftung, Kühlung und Sanitär: Frei+Partner Haustechnikplanung AG
Bauphysik: Gartenmann Engineering AG
Projektleiterin: Bianca Kilian
Mitarbeit: Panagiota Sarantinoudi

Direct contract
Construction: 2017–2019
Client: I+B Baechi Foundation
Civil engineer: Born Partner AG
Heating, ventilation, air conditioning and plumbing: Frei+Partner Haustechnikplanung AG
Building physics: Gartenmann Engineering AG
Project manager: Bianca Kilian
Team: Panagiota Sarantinoudi

107

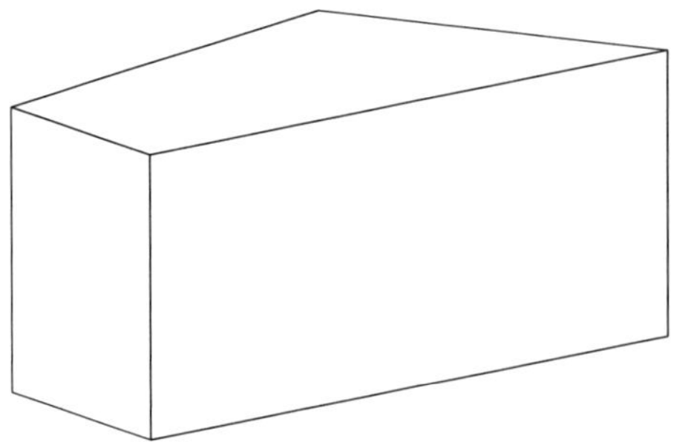

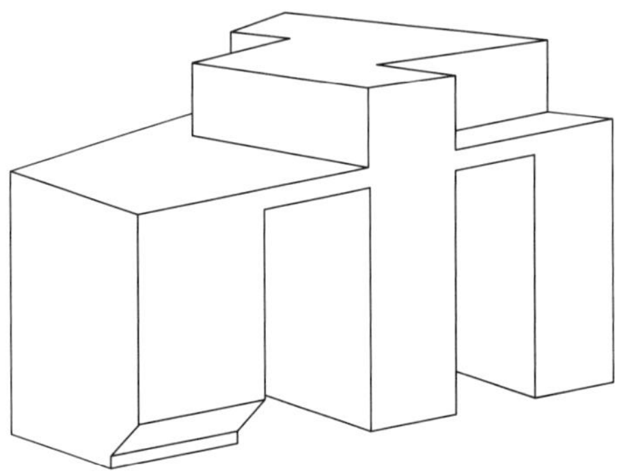

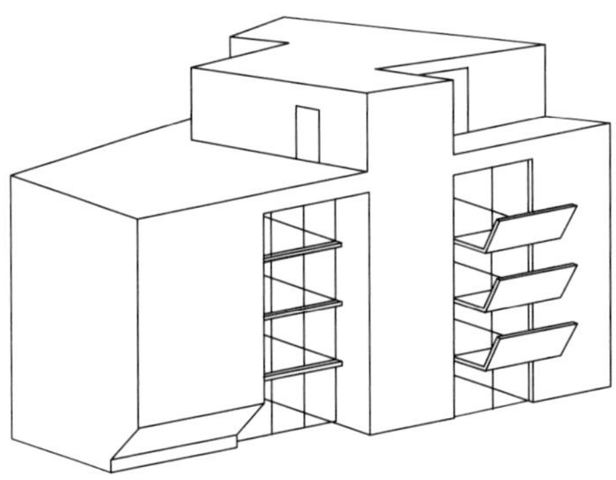

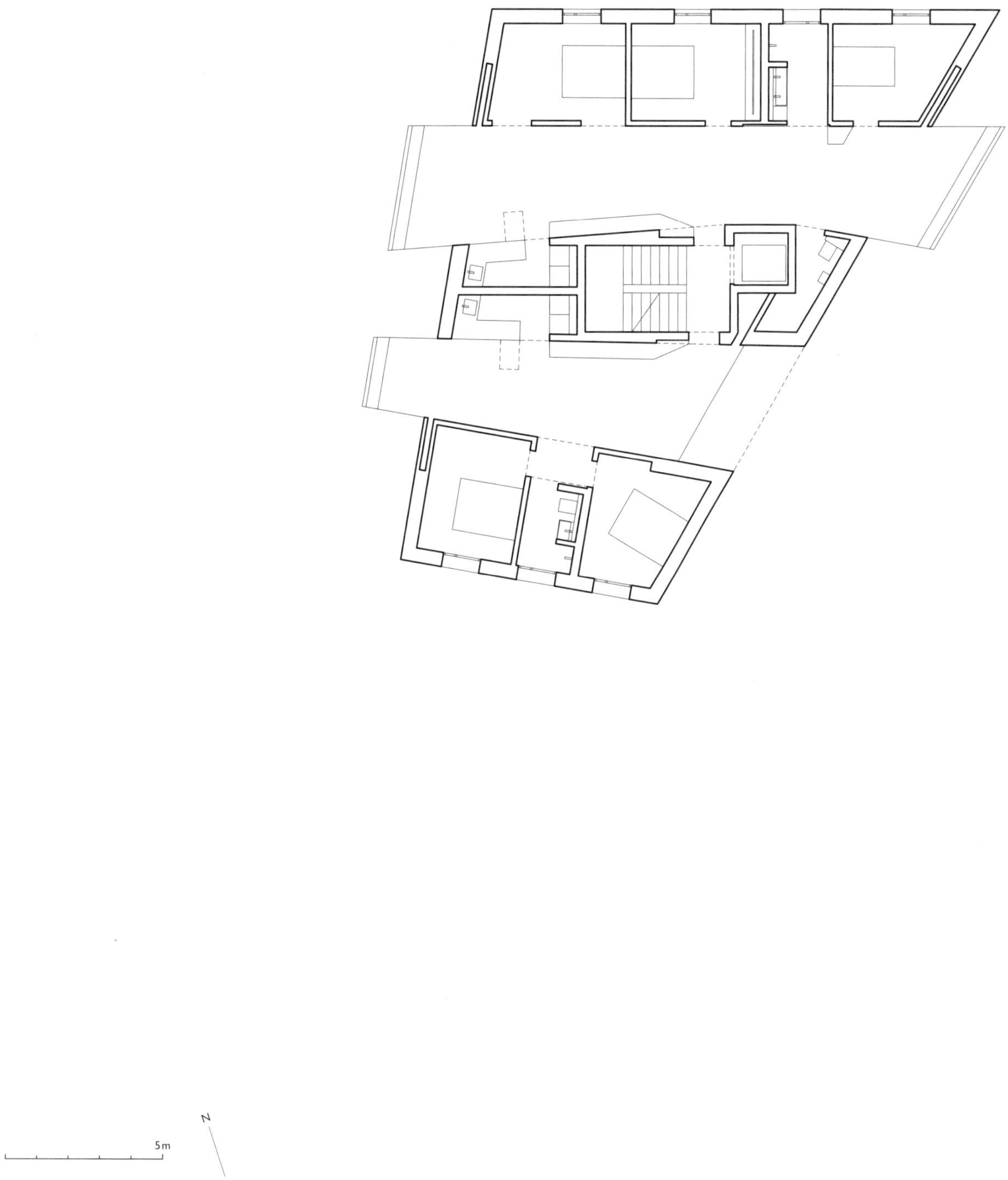
5m
N

Das sogenannte Pavillon-Haus mit markanter Dachlandschaft ist von der ruralen Architektur und insbesondere von den Bauernhäusern seiner Umgebung inspiriert. Im idyllischen Buchberg gelegen, besteht der Neubau aus (recyceltem) Beton und lokalem Holz. Diese simple Materialpalette findet Resonanz in den einfachen geometrischen Formen. Während der Sockel komplett aus Beton besteht, wurde das Obergeschoss mit den Schlafzimmern ausschliesslich in Holz errichtet. Das tragende Betonskelett trägt das vorkonstruierte Holzdach, das durch seine imposanten Dimensionen an eine Scheune erinnert. Im Erdgeschoss mit offenem Wohnbereich erlauben mehrere hölzerne Schiebefenster eine flexible Nutzung des freien Grundrisses. An warmen Tagen verdoppelt sich die vom Dach geschützte Fläche, weil ein beachtlicher Teil des Erdgeschosses als Aussenraum konzipiert ist. Durch diese gedeckte Terrasse verbindet sich der Wohnbereich unkompliziert und unmittelbar mit seiner Umgebung. Hierarchien existieren in dieser Architektur nicht, weder im Hinblick auf die Materialisierung noch die Ästhetik und schon gar nicht auf die speziell ausgebildeten Zonen: Einerseits vermittelt die als Betontopografie realisierte Sitzlandschaft an der peripheren Mauer zwischen Innen und Aussen, anderseits ist der Raum als fliessendes Kontinuum ohne permanente Grenzen gestaltet.

The building known as "The Pavilion House" has a striking roof landscape and is inspired by rural architecture and especially by the farmhouses in the vicinity. Situated in the idyllic Buchberg region, the new building is made of (recycled) concrete and local wood. This reduced range of materials resonates with the simple geometric forms. While the plinth section is completely made of concrete, the upper level accommodating the bedrooms was exclusively constructed in wood. The load-bearing concrete skeleton supports the prefabricated wooden roof, which is reminiscent of a barn due to its impressive dimensions. On the ground floor with an open living area, several wooden sliding windows enable flexible utilisation of the open floor plan. On warm days, the roof-covered area is doubled, since a considerable proportion of the ground floor is conceived as an exterior space. This covered patio connects the living area to the exterior space in an uncomplicated, direct way. No hierarchies exist in this architecture with respect to the materialisation and the aesthetics, and certainly to the specially developed zones: firstly, the seating landscape along the peripheral wall, which was implemented as a concrete topography, mediates between indoor and outdoor areas. Secondly, the space is designed as a fluent continuum without permanent boundaries.

Direktauftrag
Ausführung: 2018–2019
Bauherrschaft: Privat
Bauingenieur: Born Partner AG
Heizung, Lüftung, Kühlung und Sanitär: Frei+Partner Haustechnikplanung AG
Bauphysik: Gartenmann Engineering AG
Projektleiterin: Bianca Kilian
Mitarbeit: Panagiota Sarantinoudi

Direct contract
Construction: 2018–2019
Client: Private
Civil engineer: Born Partner AG
Heating, ventilation, air conditioning and plumbing: Frei+Partner Haustechnikplanung AG
Building physics: Gartenmann Engineering AG
Project manager: Bianca Kilian
Team: Panagiota Sarantinoudi

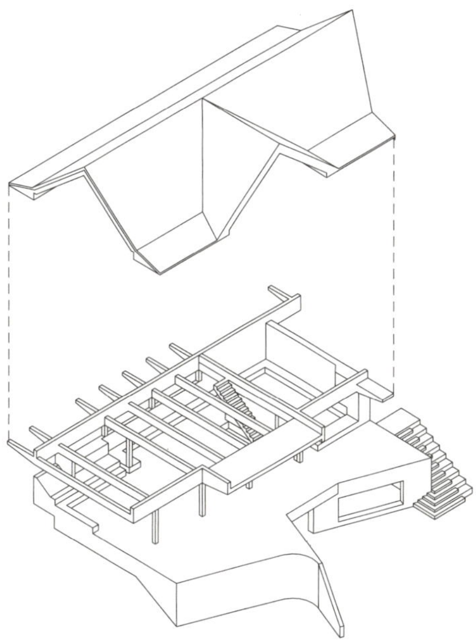

Reduzierte Volumen prägen die im Aufriss trichterförmige Can Jungla. Die begrünten Dachterrassen der beiden axialsymmetrisch entworfenen Wohnbauten, die nur durch einen Sockel miteinander verbunden sind, werden von einer zweigeschossigen Sichtbetonstruktur getragen. Sie enthält alle Installationen und bestimmt das architektonische Erscheinungsbild massgeblich. In die mit Schalungsspuren versehene, imposant wirkende Tragstruktur sind braune Holzmodule mit Balkonen eingelassen, die in ihrer Leichtigkeit die kompakte Masse des hellen Betons kontrastieren. Farblich harmonieren die ausdrucksstarken und unkaschierten Materialien perfekt. Die unterschiedlichen, aber immer grossformatigen Glasfronten lassen sich durch mehrere Faltschiebefenster und -türen unkompliziert und einfach öffnen. Innen und aussen durchdringen sich, der fliessende Wohnbereich verbindet sich nahtlos mit dem Aussenraum. Diese Flächen sind individuell bespielbar, feste Grenzen wurden maximal eliminiert. Fixe Einrichtungen, die ein spezifisches Programm voraussetzen, befinden sich peripher angeordnet. Fast schon skulptural lesen sich die Aufbauten auf den Flachdächern. Deren akkurate Formen muten vor der üppigen mediterranen Pflanzenkulisse besonders streng an – doch in der archaischen Ästhetik ist die Architektur mit der Natur vereint.

Reduced volumes define the Can Jungla with its funnel-shaped floor plan. The green rooftop terraces of the two residential buildings were designed axisymmetrically, are joined by a common plinth and are supported by a two-storey exposed-concrete structure. It contains all installations and defines the architectural appearance. Brown wooden modules with balconies have been inserted into the impressive-looking load-bearing structure, which reveals its formwork marks. The modules' lightness contrast with the compact mass of the light-coloured concrete. The colours of the expressive, exposed materials harmonise perfectly. The different, but always large-scale glass fronts are easily opened by means of several folding, sliding windows. Interior and exterior spaces interpenetrate, while the fluent living area smoothly connects with the outdoor environment. These areas can be utilised individually, as fixed boundaries were kept to a minimum. Permanent fittings reflecting a specific programme are arranged peripherally. The structures on the flat roofs can almost be read as sculptural. Their accurate forms appear especially stringent in front of the lush green Mediterranean backdrop – yet the architecture is still united with the environment through its archaic aesthetics.

Direktauftrag: 2023
Ausführung: 2024–2026
Bauherrschaft: Privat
Mitarbeit: Andre Sashko

Direct contract: 2023
Construction: 2024–2026
Client: Private
Team: Andre Sashko

Der Bahnhof Herrliberg-Feldmeilen bildet einen neuen Netzknotenpunkt, einen wichtigen Bestandteil des komplexen Verkehrssystems. Entlang der Gleise sind das Aufnahmegebäude, der Güterschuppen und mehrere Wohnbauten auf einem terrassenartigen Plateau mit Seepanorama angeordnet. Sie unterscheiden sich durch differenziert gestaltete Fassaden und vielseitige Volumina. Mit einem hohen Anteil an Recyclingbeton und regionalem Holz ist die Bauweise konsequent hybrid gehalten. Die rohe Materialisierung ist nicht nur ästhetisch und ökonomisch motiviert, sondern entspringt auch nachhaltigen Forderungen. Seiner städtebaulichen Bedeutung entsprechend bildet der prägnante Aufnahmekomplex den markanten Auftakt zum neuen Ensemble. Dieses schafft durch intelligente Setzungen diverse Raumpassagen und Blickachsen. Miteinander verbundene Freiräume und grüne Oasen mit grossen Bäumen, aber auch ein Spielplatz und kollektive Dachterrassen bieten hohe Aufenthaltsqualitäten. Generell ist das Bahnhofsareal als dynamische Plattform konzipiert, die frische Synergien kreieren soll. So sind die strassenseitig orientierten Erdgeschosse meist frei bespielbar und offerieren flexible Nutzungspotenziale für gemeinschaftliche Orte, Restaurants oder Shops. Gleichzeitig kann der Freiraum als Fest- und Marktplatz dienen.

Herrliberg-Feldmeilen Station creates a new network hub, making it an important element of the complex transport system. Along the tracks, the reception building, the freight shed and several residential buildings are arranged on a terrace-like plateau with a panoramic view of the lake. They are distinguished by the differentiated design of their façades and the many-sided volumes. The construction method's high proportion of recycled concrete and regional wood makes it consistently hybrid. The raw materialisation is not only motivated by aesthetics and economics, but also takes sustainability demands into account. Reflecting its urban-planning importance, the concise reception complex forms the striking beginning of the new ensemble. Its intelligent placement achieves diverse spatial passages and visual axes. Interconnected open spaces and green oases with large trees, as well as a playground and collective rooftop terraces, offer high qualities of stay. Generally, the station grounds are conceived as a dynamic platform aimed at creating fresh synergies. Thus the ground floors facing the street are mostly freely definable and offer flexible use potential for communal spaces, restaurants or shops. At the same time, the open space can be used as a square for festivals and markets.

Wettbewerb: 2021, 1. Preis
Ausführung: 2026–2030
Bauherrschaft: SBB Immobilien
In Zusammenarbeit mit:
Hosoya Schaefer Architects AG
Bauingenieur: Dr. Lüchinger+Meyer Bauingenieure AG
Landschaftsarchitektur: S2L Landschaftsarchitekten BSLA
Mitarbeit: Nerea Aranzabal, Giorgio Fontana, Mélanie Jeannet, Bianca Kilian, Ekaterina Nagibina-François

Competition: 2021, 1st Prize
Construction: 2026–2030
Client: SBB Immobilien
In collaboration with:
Hosoya Schaefer Architects AG
Civil engineer: Dr. Lüchinger+Meyer Bauingenieure AG
Landscape architecture: S2L Landschaftsarchitekten BSLA
Team: Nerea Aranzabal, Giorgio Fontana, Mélanie Jeannet, Bianca Kilian, Ekaterina Nagibina-François

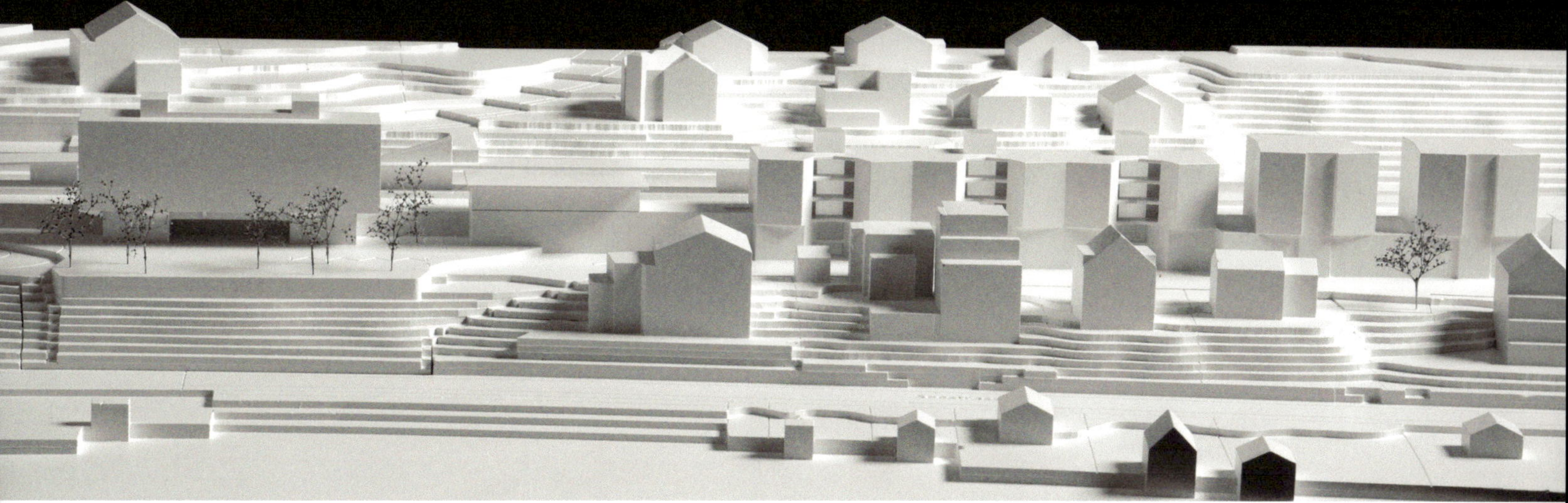

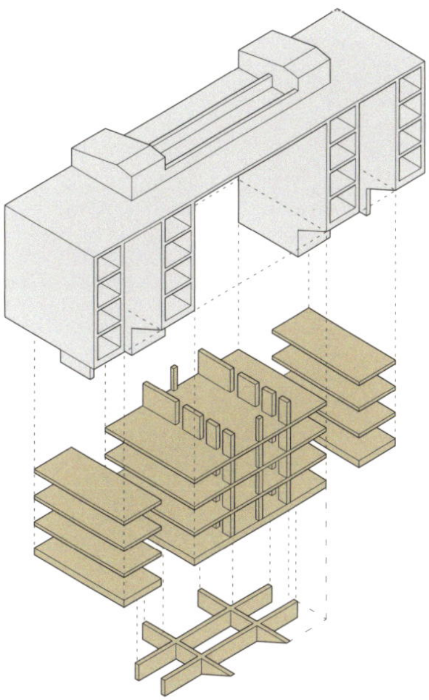

CFF FFS

Das nutzungsdurchmischte Ensemble des Zentrums Affoltern besteht aus einem Hochhaus, das sich als städtische Landmarke präsentiert, einem daran anschliessenden L-förmigen Volumen sowie einer separaten Quartieranlage. Die Bauten sind intelligent positioniert und spannen einen allseitig offenen, begrünten Platz auf. Generell greifen Innen und Aussen im Sinne eines organisch aufgefassten Raumkontinuums ineinander, zudem sind die Erdgeschosse integrativ und kommunikativ gestaltet. Die von präzisen Geometrien gezeichnete Architektur tritt mit ihrem gestaffelten Massstab in einen Dialog mit dem bebauten Kontext. Kolonnaden, Sitztribünen und Vordächer schaffen clevere Verbindungen zur Umgebung. Plastizität verleihen die hölzernen Streben, die zugleich horizontale Akzente setzen. Als Band angeordnete Loggien bringen Tiefe in die ebenen, von einem orthogonalen Holzraster gerahmten Fassaden. Die Farbgebung ist dezent gehalten. In ihrer verschiedenartigen Gestaltung suggerieren kollektiv nutzbare Terrassen eine luftige Leichtigkeit – die filigranen Konstruktionen, die mit geraden, geknickten und gerundeten Formen abschliessen und sich mit Textil bespannen lassen, heben sich als elegante Dachkronen ab. Die kompakten, unterschiedlichen Wohntypologien sind modulartig konzipiert und erlauben ein «Wohnkontinnum» von Süden nach Norden.

The mixed-use ensemble of Affoltern Centre consists of a high-rise building that presents itself as an urban landmark, an adjoining L-shaped volume and a separate residential estate. The buildings are intelligently positioned and span a green square that is open on all sides. Generally, interior and exterior areas interpenetrate in the sense of an organically grasped spatial continuum, while the ground floors are designed to be integrative and communicative. Characterised by precise geometries, the architecture's staggered scale enters into a dialogue with the developed context. Colonnades, seating stands and canopies create clever connections to the surroundings. The wooden struts add a sculptural quality, while providing horizontal accentuation. Loggias arranged as a band add depth to the even façades framed by an orthogonal wooden grid. The colour scheme is reserved. In their diverse design, the collectively usable terraces suggest an airy lightness. The intricate roof structures, which are concluded by straight, kinked and rounded forms and can be covered with textiles, set themselves apart as elegant crowning elements on the roof. The compact, diverse housing typologies are conceived in a modular way and enable "continuous living" from south to north.

Wettbewerb: 2022, 2. Preis
Bauherrschaft: Migros-Pensionskasse und Post Immobilien
In Zusammenarbeit mit:
HHF Architekten
Bauingenieur: Dr. Lüchinger+Meyer Bauingenieure AG
Landschaftsarchitektur:
SIMA|BREER Landschaftsarchitektur
Mitarbeit: Bianca Arciero, Bianca Kilian, Nerea Aranzabal, Eva Razloznik

Competition 2022, 2nd Prize
Client: Migros-Pensionskasse and Post Immobilien
In collaboration with:
HHF Architekten
Civil engineer: Dr. Lüchinger+Meyer Bauingenieure AG
Landscape architecture:
SIMA | BREER Landschaftsarchitektur
Team: Bianca Arciero, Bianca Kilian, Nerea Aranzabal, Eva Razloznik

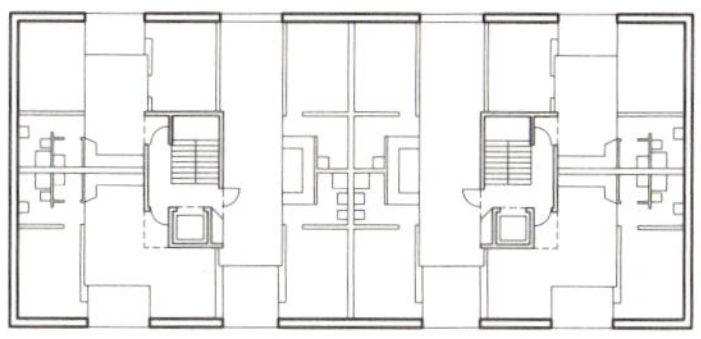

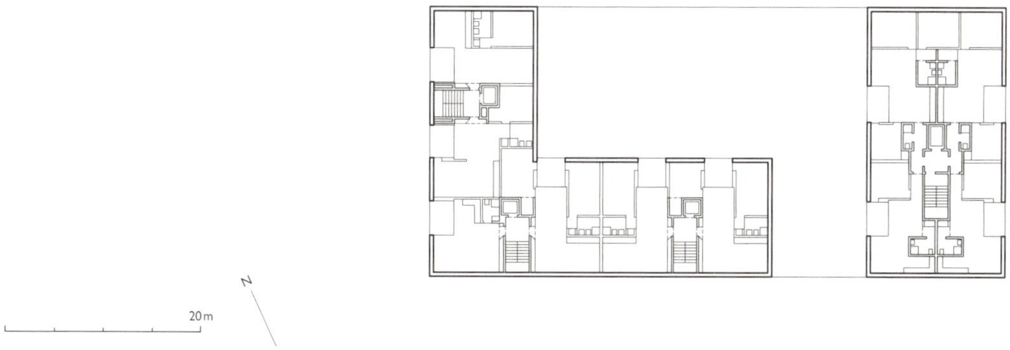
N
20 m

DEMNAS ATELIER UND BFRNDS STUDIO, CHÂTEL-SAINT-DENIS

DEMNA'S ATELIER AND BFRND'S STUDIO, CHÂTEL-SAINT-DENIS

In eine sanfte Hanglage gesetzt, liest sich die Architektur als moderne Interpretation alpiner Baukultur: Das markante, geneigte Dach, das der Topografie folgt, und die fein gegliederte Holzfassade stellen im schweizerischen Berggebiet typische Merkmale dar. Ist das Gebäude in seiner Aussengestaltung harmonisch in den ruralen Kontext eingebettet, so entfaltet sich im Innern eine komplexe Struktur, die in ihrer Materialisierung – poröser bis grobkörniger Sichtbeton – zwar einen dezidierten Kontrast zum äusseren Erscheinungsbild setzt, aber dennoch Assoziationen an die brachiale, steinige Gebirgswelt weckt. Die Betontopografie besticht durch diverse Ebenen und bietet unterschiedliche Sitzgelegenheiten, ausserdem verbindet sie sich durch eine lang gezogene Fensterfront gegen Osten souverän mit dem Aussenraum. Eine kreisrunde Möblierung in der Mitte des offenen Wohnzimmers markiert symbolisch das soziale Zentrum. Flexibilität ist trotz der fixen Betonlandschaft gegeben: Der innere Wohnbereich lässt sich durch Schiebetüren oder Vorhänge problemlos von der Terrasse im Freien abtrennen. Das minimalistisch gehaltene Bad ohne aufdringliche Armaturen erinnert fast schon an eine Grotte. Generell wird das gestalterische Konzept von einer reduzierten, aber ausdrucksstark anmutenden Ästhetik bestimmt.

Placed on a gentle slope, the architecture reads as a modern interpretation of Alpine building culture: the prominent slanting roof, which follows the line of the terrain, and the finely structured wooden façade represent typical features of the Swiss mountain region. While the building's outward appearance is harmoniously embedded in the rural context, a complex structure unfolds inside. Its materialisation – porous to coarse-grained exposed concrete – contrasts markedly with the exterior appearance, but nevertheless inspires associations with a powerful, rocky mountain environment. The concrete topography is distinctive through diverse levels and offers a variety of seating opportunities. It also confidently connects with the exterior space with its long eastward-facing window front. Circular furniture in the middle of the open living room symbolically marks the social centre. Flexibility is still ensured despite the fixed concrete landscape: the inner living area can easily be partitioned from the open-air terrace by means of sliding doors or curtains. The minimalist bathroom without overt fittings almost resembles a grotto. Generally, the design concept is determined by aesthetics of reduced, yet powerfully expressive appearances.

Direktauftrag
Bauherrschaft: Demna Gvasalia, Loïck Gomez
Bauingenieur: Dr. Lüchinger+Meyer Bauingenieure AG
Heizung, Lüftung, Kühlung und Sanitär: Energie Concept S.A.
Bauphysik: Gartenmann Engineering AG
Projektleiterin: Nerea Aranzabal
Mitarbeit: Bianca Arciero

Direct contract
Client: Demna Gvasalia, Loïck Gomez
Civil engineer: Dr. Lüchinger+Meyer Bauingenieure AG
Heating, ventilation, air conditioning and plumbing: Energie Concept S.A.
Building physics: Gartenmann Engineering AG
Project manager: Nerea Aranzabal
Team: Bianca Arciero

UMBAU PODERE LARIGNANO, FAUGLIA

RESTORATION OF THE PODERE LARIGNANO, FAUGLIA

Das idyllisch gelegene Landhaus ist von weiten Feldern umgeben und präsentiert sich mit einer kronenartigen Dachterrasse in majestätisch-anmutiger Manier. Dieser Charakter findet sich auch im Innern wieder – es ist ein prägnanter Ausdruck, den es beim Umbau unbedingt zu sichern galt. So sind die Interventionen reduziert und punktuell gehalten, doch gerade dadurch intensivieren sie die besondere Atmosphäre der Architektur: Sanfte Betonpartien kontrastieren die grobe Haptik des Bruchsteinmauerwerks, und orthogonale Formen setzten präzise Gegenakzente zu den alten Mauern mit ihren oftmals rau wirkenden Texturen. Durch die neu geschaffene Sichtbetonstruktur im peripheren Raum ergeben sich mehrere Sitzgelegenheiten. Gleichzeitig resultieren daraus markante lineare Rahmungen von grossem visuellem Reiz. Dazu tragen auch die hochrechteckigen Fenster mit hellbraunen Holzfassungen bei. Die modernen Elemente integrieren sich überall harmonisch in die bestehende Farb- und Materialpalette. Zum Teil sind sie aber auch auf Dualität angelegt – glatt und uneben, kantig und rund sind Dichotomien, die mehrfach vorkommen. Das fliessende Innenraumkonzept mit Enfiladen nimmt die malerische Weite der toskanischen Natur auf. Ein Pool und diverse Gartenmauern führen die Betontopografie im Aussenbereich fort.

At its idyllic location surrounded by broad fields, the country house presents itself in a regal manner with a crowning rooftop terrace. This character is also continued in the interior – with a concise expression that absolutely had to be preserved during the conversion measures. Thus, the interventions were reduced and isolated, although in fact these intensify the special atmosphere of the architecture: gentle concrete sections contrast with the coarse feel of the dry-stone wall, while orthogonal forms add precise contrary accentuation to the old walls with their often rough textures. The newly created exposed-concrete structure in the peripheral space provides additional seating. At the same time, this produces striking and highly attractive linear framing. The portrait-format windows with light brown wooden frames are also contributing factors. Everywhere, the modern elements are harmoniously integrated into the existing range of colours and materials. However, some of them reflect the duality of their design, with recurring dichotomies of smooth and uneven, and angular and round. The fluent interior spatial concept with enfilades picks up on the picturesque expanse of the Tuscan countryside. A pool and various garden furniture elements continue the concrete topography in the outdoor space.

Direktauftrag
Ausführung: 2023–2025
Bauherrschaft: Privat
Bauingenieur: Andrea D'Angelo Ingenere
Projektleiterin: Bianca Arciero
Mitarbeit: Giorgio Fontana

Direct contract
Construction: 2023–2025
Client: Private
Civil engineer: Andrea D'Angelo Ingenere
Project manager: Bianca Arciero
Team: Giorgio Fontana

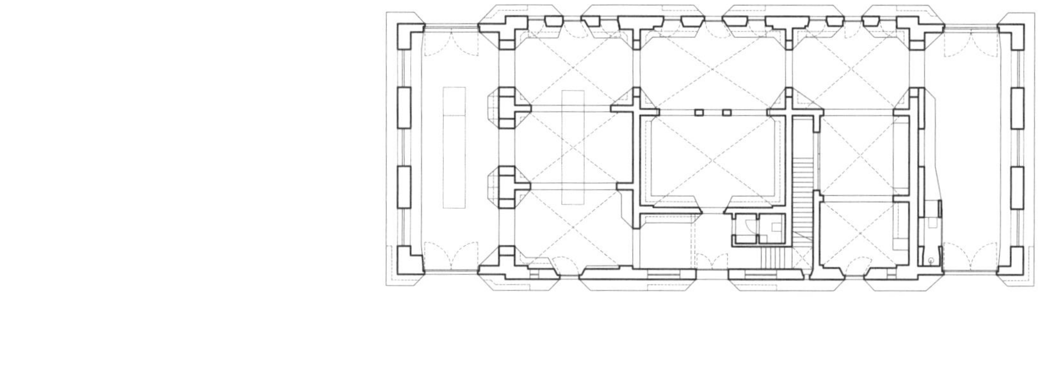
10m
N

WERKVERZEICHNIS
Auswahl Bauten, Projekte und Wettbewerbe

2004		Umbau Loft «The Glacier», Luzern
		Umbau Mehrfamilienhaus G6, Zürich
		Wohn- und Geschäftshaus Cedrus, Meilen
	1	Aspecta-Versicherungsbüros, Hamburg
2005	2	Strandhaus, Goa
2006		Bürogebäude TBWA, Zürich
2008		Bar 0815, Zürich
		Mediaxis Media Lab, Schlieren
		Studentenhotel Melon District, Barcelona
		Feldbalz House, Herrliberg
2009		Umbau Crusch Alba, Barcelona
2011		Wettbewerb Schulhaus, Allschwil
	3	Studie MFH, Herrliberg
2012		Residenz Los Limoneros, Marbella
		Residenz 2 Verandas, Erlenbach
		Wettbewerb Green-Square-Bibliothek und Plaza, Sydney
		Innenumbau Wintergarten Landhaus, Buchberg
	4	Studie Einfamilienhaus vRm, Zumikon
2012–2017	5	Landhaus, Ses Salines, Mallorca
2013		Wettbewerb Wohnüberbauung Labitzke, Zürich
		Studienauftrag Hotel Mondrian, Paris
2014		Inselresort Moskito, British Virgin Islands
		Umbau Mehrfamilienhaus, Andeer
		Umbau Wohngebäude G20, Zürich
		Mehrfamilienhaus Stone H, Zürich
		Landhaus, Santanyí, Mallorca
2014–2017		Umbau Mehrfamilienhaus Z22 und F88, Zürich
2015		Wettbewerb Bauhaus Museum, Dessau
	6	Wettbewerb Wien Museum neu (Finalist)
		Umbau Wohnung Löwenbräuareal, Zürich
2016		Mehrfamilienhaus Magliaso, Ticino
		Mehrfamilienhaus, Zürich-Zollikon
		Wettbewerb Neue Nationalgalerie, Berlin
2017	7	Wettbewerb sozialer Wohnungsbau Hardau, Zürich
2018	8	Wettbewerb Haus Eber, Wohnen für junge Erwachsene in Ausbildung, Zürich-Aussersihl
2019		Das Pavillon-Haus, Buchberg
		Studie Mehrfamilienhaus, Buch am Irchel
		Wettbewerb Genossenschaftswohnungen Freihampton, München
	9	Wettbewerb neuer Forschungscampus für die Chernovetsky-Stiftung, Kiew (2. Preis)
	10	Wettbewerb Mehrfamilienhaus Heuteil, Bad Ragaz
		Bezahlbarer Wohnraum für alle, Langgrütstrasse, Zürich
2020		Mehrfamilienhaus, Buch am Irchel
2021		Studie Mehrfamilienhaus, Trüllikon
		Wettbewerb Wohnhaus Burgfelderstrasse, Basel
		Mehrfamilienhaus Neftenbach, Zürich
2022	11	Wettbewerb Ersatzneubau Zypressenstrasse, Winterthur
	12	Wettbewerb Bahnhofsareal Wollishofen, Zürich
	13	Wettbewerb Zentrum Zürich-Affoltern (2. Preis)

		Laufende Projekte:
	14	Bahnhof Herrliberg-Feldmeilen (Wettbewerb 2021, 1. Preis)
		Umbau Podere Larignano, Fauglia, Toskana
		Demnas Atelier und BFRNDs Studio, Châtel-Saint-Denis
	15	Demnas Industrielles Atelier, Cala Murada, Manacor, Mallorca
		2 Berghäuser, Juf
		Can Bosc i Platja, Santanyí, Mallorca
		Landhaus Possessió E, Santanyí, Mallorca
		Landhaus Possessió N, Santanyí, Mallorca
		Landhaus Possessió W, Santanyí, Mallorca
		Landhaus Possessió al Turo, Ses Salines, Mallorca
		Landhaus Villa Aumallia, Felanitx, Mallorca (Studie 2018)
		Can Jungla, Santanyí, Mallorca
		Umbau Wohnung Germaniastrasse, Zürich
	16	Landhaus Ses Mires, Santanyí, Mallorca
		Landhaus Son Gelabert, Felanitx, Mallorca
		Studie Mehrfamilienhaus Winterthurerstrasse, Zürich

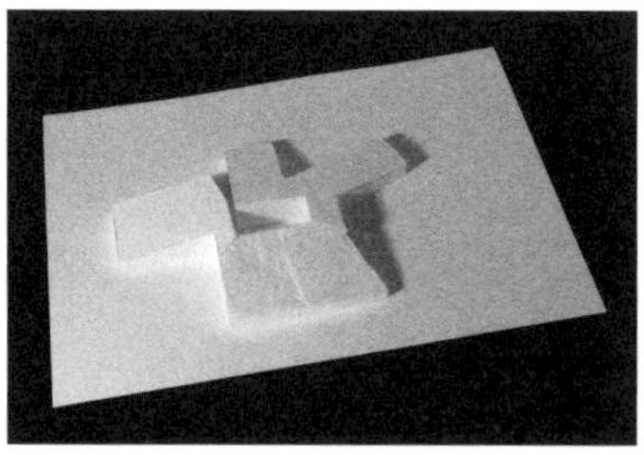
5

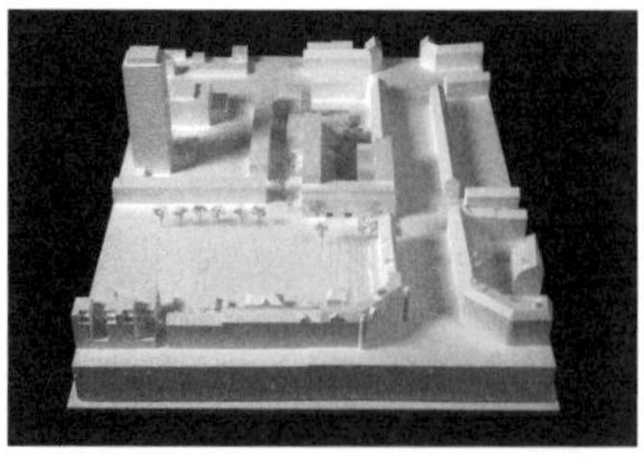
7

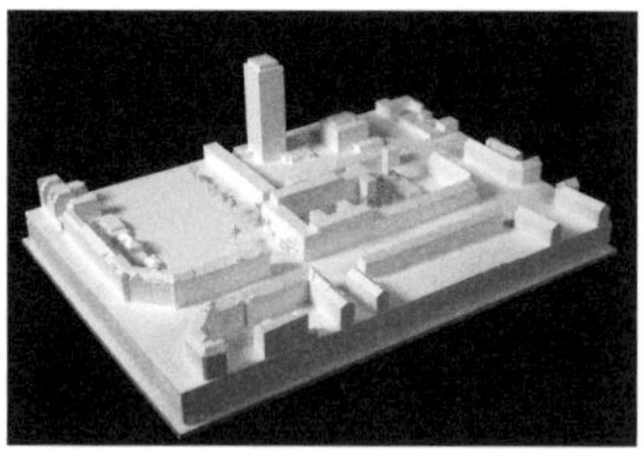
7

13

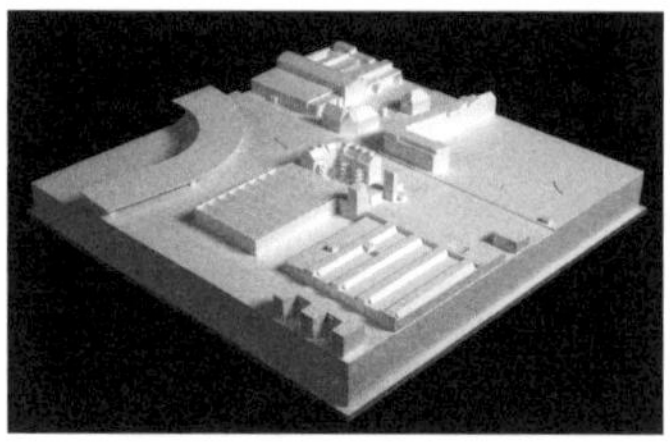
8

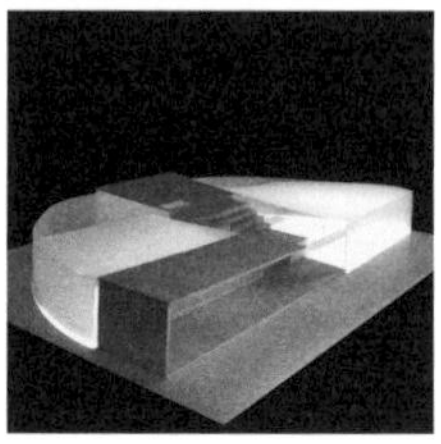
2

15

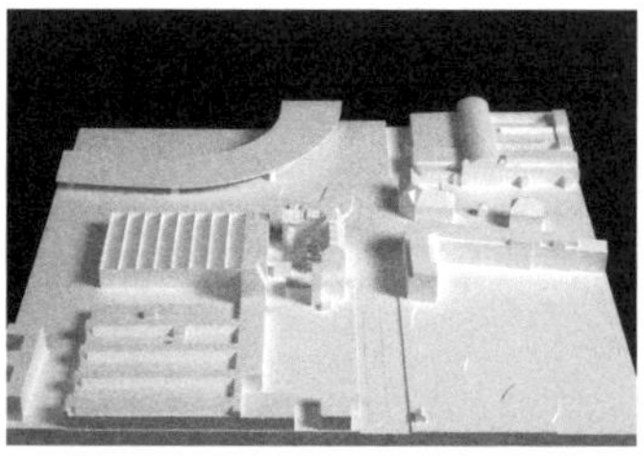
8

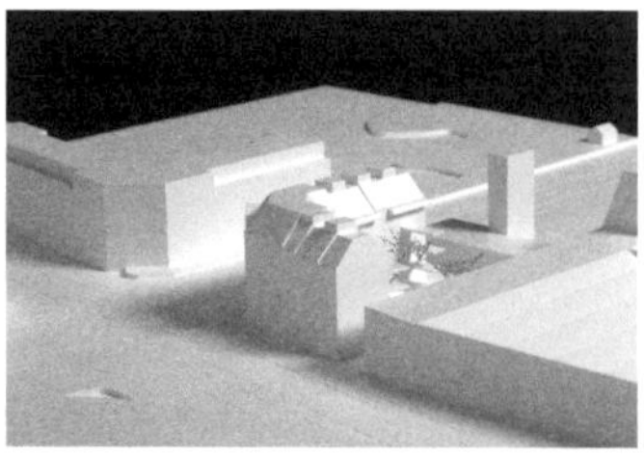
8

16

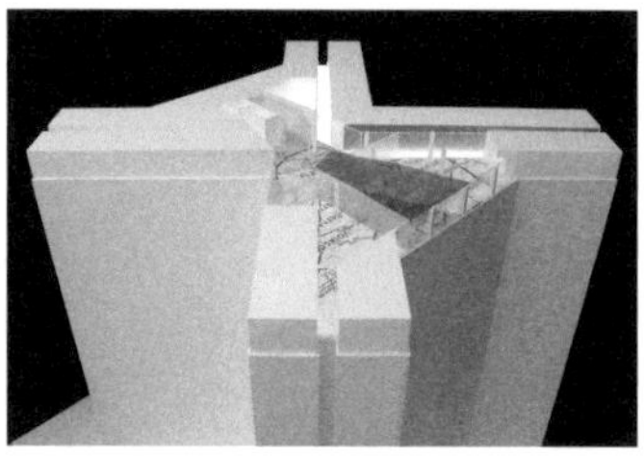
1

10

10

11

1

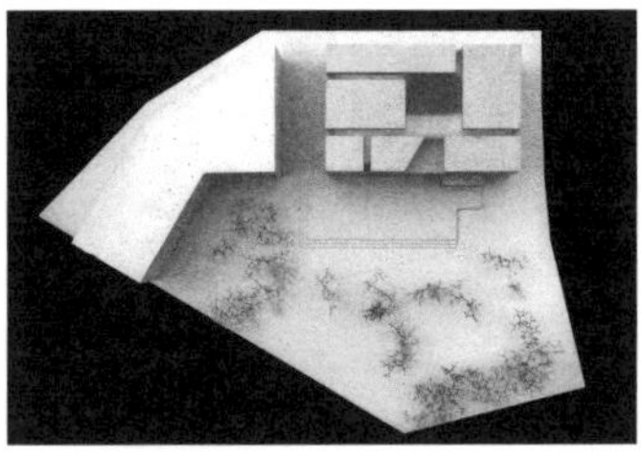

6

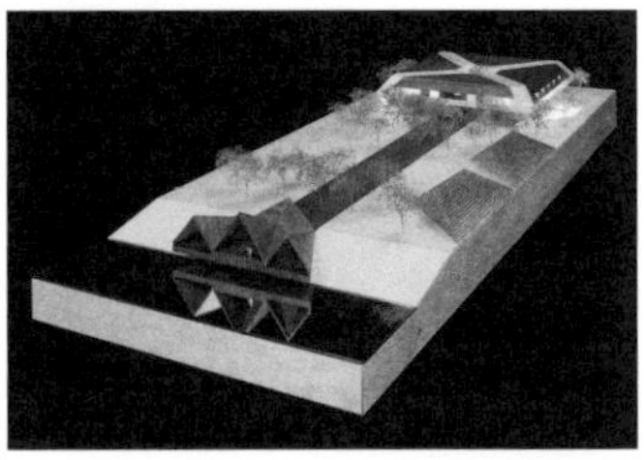

9

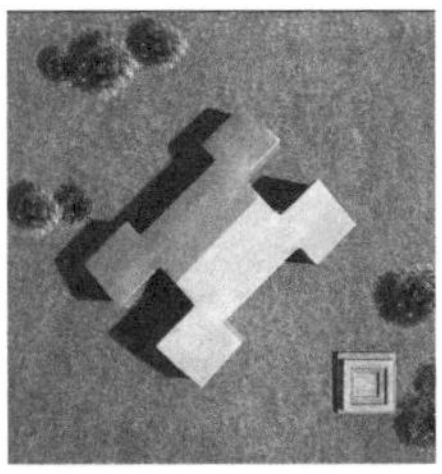

16

9

9

16

9

5

5

14

3

12

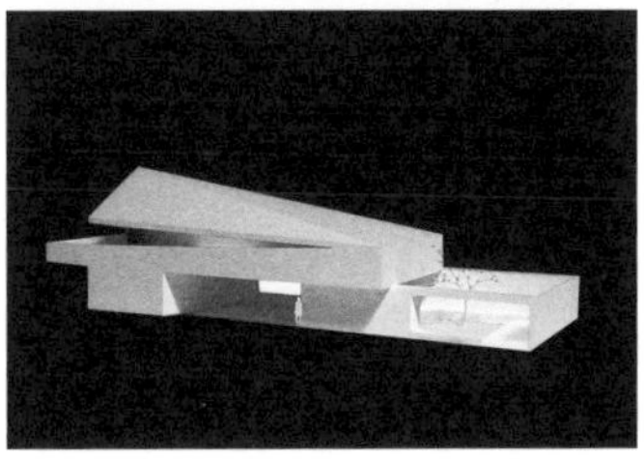

4

LIST OF WORKS

Selection of buildings, projects and competitions

2004		Conversion, "The Glacier" loft, Lucerne
		Conversion, G6 apartment building, Zurich
		Cedrus residential and office building, Meilen
	1	Aspecta insurance offices, Hamburg
2005	2	Beach house, Goa
2006		TBWA office building, Zurich
2008		Bar 0815, Zurich
		Mediaxis Media Lab, Schlieren
		Student hotel, Melon District, Barcelona
		Feldbalz House, Herrliberg
2009		Conversion, Crusch Alba, Barcelona
2011		Competition, school, Allschwil
	3	Study, apartment building, Herrliberg
2012		Los Limoneros residence, Marbella
		2 Verandas residence, Erlenbach
		Competition, Green Square Library and Plaza, Sydney
		Interior conversion, country house winter garden, Buchberg
	4	Study, vRm single-family home, Zumikon
2012–2017	5	Country house, Ses Salines, Mallorca
2013		Competition, Labitzke housing, Zurich
		Contracted study, Hotel Mondrian, Paris
2014		Moskito Island resort, British Virgin Islands
		Renovation, apartment building, Andeer
		Renovation, G20 residential building, Zurich
		Stone H apartment building, Zurich
		Country house, Santanyí, Mallorca
2014–2017		House Z22 and warehouse F88, Zurich
2015		Competition, Bauhaus Museum, Dessau
	6	New Vienna Museum (Finalist)
		Conversion, Löwenbräuareal apartment, Zurich
2016		Apartment building, Magliaso, Ticino
		Apartment building, Zurich-Zollikon
		Competition, New National Gallery, Berlin
2017	7	Competition, Hardau social housing, Zurich
2018	8	Competition, Eber House, housing for young adults in vocational training, Zurich-Aussersihl
2019		The Pavilion House, Buchberg
		Study, apartment building, Buch am Irchel
		Competition, Freihampton cooperative housing, Munich
	9	Competition, new research campus for the Chernovetsky Foundation, Kiev (2nd Prize)
	10	Competition, Heuteil apartment building, Bad Ragaz
		Affordable housing for all, Langgrütstrasse, Zurich
2020		Apartment building, Buch am Irchel
2021		Study, apartment building, Trüllikon
		Competition, Burgfelderstrasse housing, Basel
		Neftenbach housing, Zurich
2022	11	Competition, replacement building, Zypressenstrasse, Winterthur
	12	Competition, Wollishofen Station area, Zurich
	13	Competition, Zurich-Affoltern centre (2nd Prize)
		Ongoing projects:
	14	Herrliberg-Feldmeilen train station (Competition in 2021, 1st Prize)
		Restoration of the Podere Larignano, Fauglia, Tuscany
		Demna's atelier and BFRND's studio, Châtel-Saint-Denis
	15	Demna's industrial studio, Cala Murada, Manacor, Mallorca
		2 Alpine houses, Juf
		Can Bosc i Platja, Santanyí, Mallorca
		Country house, Possessió E, Santanyí, Mallorca
		Country house, Possessió N, Santanyí, Mallorca
		Country house, Possessió W, Santanyí, Mallorca
		Country house, Possessió al Turo, Ses Salines, Mallorca
		Villa Aumallia country house, Felanitx, Mallorca (study in 2018)
		Can Jungla, Santanyí, Mallorca
		Renovation, Germaniastrasse apartment, Zurich
	16	Country house, Ses Mires, Santanyí, Mallorca
		Country house, Son Gelabert, Felanitx, Mallorca
		Study, Winterthurerstrasse apartment building, Zurich

GUS WÜSTEMANN

1966	Geboren in Zürich
1988–1995	Architekturstudium ETH Zürich
1994	Auslandsemester in Ahmedabad, Indien
1995	Diplom, ETH Zürich
1996	Gründung Gus Wüstemann Architekten AG in Zürich
2004	Büro in Barcelona
2010	Mitgründer und Kurator von catalan-architects.com
2018	Mitglied Beirat der Stadt Barcelona
2019	Büro in Cala Figuera, Mallorca

TEAM

aktuell	Nerea Aranzabal, Bianca Arciero, Amalia Granolleras, Bianca Kilian, Chiara Wüstemann, Maria Wüstemann, BTO
ehemalig	Nadia Campos, Giorgio Fontana, Marta Balsera Goni, Hector Gonzalez, Manuel Greter, Rodrigo Iturrieta, Valentin Kokudev, Jan Kubasiewicz, Mariana Marques da Silva, Andre Müller, Ronny Ott, Eftychia Pathanasiou, Daniel Pelach, Silvia Pujalte, Javier Cort Roselló, Panagiota Sarantinoudi, Andre Sashko, Jürg Spahr, Alexander Thieme, Bahare Torbati

AUSZEICHNUNGEN

2007	*Record Interiors, Architectural Record:* Umbau Loft «The Glacier», Luzern
2010	*Contractworld Award* (Kategorie Büro): Mediaxis Media Lab, Schlieren
	Record Interiors, Architectural Record: Umbau Crusch Alba, Barcelona
2012	*AIT-Award, Wohnen Interior:* Umbau Crusch Alba, Barcelona
2013	*Record Houses, Architectural Record:* Residenz 2 Verandas, Erlenbach
	Best Architects 12 (Kategorie Innenarchitektur): Umbau Crusch Alba, Barcelona
	Best Architects 12 (Kategorie Wohnbauten): Umbau Crusch Alba, Barcelona
2014	*Architekurpreis der Reiners Stiftung:* Residenz 2 Verandas, Erlenbach
2015	*Record Houses, Architectural Record:* Residenz Los Limoneros, Marbella
2016	*Best Architect 2016:* Residenz Los Limoneros, Marbella
2019	*Architizer A+Awards:* Bezahlbarer Wohnraum für alle, Langgrütstrasse, Zürich
	Best Architects 20 (Gold): Bezahlbarer Wohnraum für alle, Langgrütstrasse, Zürich
	Dezeen Awards: Bezahlbarer Wohnraum für alle, Langgrütstrasse, Zürich
	Dedalo Minosse International Prize for Commissioning a Building: Bezahlbarer Wohnraum für alle, Langgrütstrasse, Zürich
2020	*AIT Award* (2. Platz; Kategorie Mehrfamilienhäuser): Bezahlbarer Wohnraum für alle, Langgrütstrasse, Zürich
2022	*Architektur Preis Kanton Zürich* (Nominierung): Bezahlbarer Wohnraum für alle, Langgrütstrasse, Zürich

AUSSTELLUNGEN

2010	*Burgauer Architekturtag,* Ulm
2016	*Total Recall* (Einzelausstellung), La Galerie d'Architecture, Paris
	Zeit – Raum – Dasein, Biennale Venedig
	Lebensräume heute, Havanna
2017	*Total Recall* (Einzelausstellung), AIT-ArchitekturSalon, Hamburg
	Total Recall (Einzelausstellung), ADC, Zürich
2023	*Mehr als gewohnt,* Vorarlberger Architektur Institut (vai), Dornbirn
2024	Architekturbiennale in Tallinn «Resources for a Future»

GUS WÜSTEMANN

1966	Born in Zurich
1988–1995	Architecture studies, ETH Zurich
1994	Exchange semester in Ahmedabad, India
1995	Graduated, ETH Zurich
1996	Founded Gus Wüstemann Architects AG in Zurich
2004	Studio in Barcelona
2010	Co-founded and curated catalan-architects.com
2018	Board member of Barcelona city council
2019	Studio in Cala Figuera, Mallorca

TEAM

current	Nerea Aranzabal, Bianca Arciero, Amalia Granolleras, Bianca Kilian, Chiara Wüstemann, Maria Wüstemann, BTO
former	Nadia Campos, Giorgio Fontana, Marta Balsera Goni, Hector Gonzalez, Manuel Greter, Rodrigo Iturrieta, Valentin Kokudev, Jan Kubasiewicz, Mariana Marques da Silva, Andre Müller, Ronny Ott, Eftychia Pathanasiou, Daniel Pelach, Silvia Pujalte, Javier Cort Roselló, Panagiota Sarantinoudi, Andre Sashko, Jürg Spahr, Alexander Thieme, Bahare Torbati

AWARDS

2007	*Record Interiors, Architectural Record:* Conversion, "The Glacier" loft, Lucerne
2010	*Contractworld Award* (Office Category): Mediaxis Media Lab, Schlieren
	Record interiors, Architectural Record: Conversion, Crusch Alba, Barcelona
2012	*AIT Award, Wohnen Interior:* Conversion, Crusch Alba, Barcelona
2013	*Record Houses, Architectural Record:* 2 Verandas residence, Erlenbach
	Best Architects 12 Award (Interior Architecture category): Conversion, Crusch Alba, Barcelona
	Best Architects 12 Award (Housing category): Conversion, Crusch Alba, Barcelona
2014	*Architectural Prize, Reiners Stiftung:* 2 Verandas residence, Erlenbach
2015	*Record Houses, Architectural Record:* Los Limoneros residence, Marbella
2016	*Best Architect 2016:* Los Limoneros residence, Marbella
2019	*Architizer A+Awards:* Affordable housing for all, Langgrütstrasse, Zurich
	Best Architects 20 (Gold Winner): Affordable housing for all, Langgrütstrasse, Zurich
	Dezeen Awards: Affordable housing for all, Langgrütstrasse, Zurich
	Dedalo Minosse International Prize for Commissioning a Building: Affordable housing for all, Langgrütstrasse, Zurich
2020	*AIT Award* (2nd Place, Multi-Family Housing Category): Affordable housing for all, Langgrütstrasse, Zurich
2022	*Architektur Preis Kanton Zürich* (nomination): Affordable housing for all, Langgrütstrasse, Zurich

EXHIBITIONS

2010	*Burgauer Architekturtag.* Ulm
2016	*Total Recall* (individual exhibition). La Galerie d'Architecture, Paris
	Time – Space – Existence. Venice Biennale
	Living Spaces Today. Havana
2017	*Total Recall* (individual exhibition). AIT-ArchitekturSalon, Hamburg
	Total Recall (individual exhibition). ADC, Zurich
2023	*Mehr als gewohnt.* Vorarlberger Architektur Institut (vai), Dornbirn
2024	Tallinn Architecture Biennale, "Resources for a Future"

FINANZIELLE UND IDEELLE UNTERSTÜTZUNG

Ein besonderer Dank gilt den Institutionen und Sponsorfirmen, deren finanzielle Unterstützungen wesentlich zum Entstehen dieser Buchreihe beitragen. Ihr kulturelles Engagement ermöglicht ein fruchtbares und freundschaftliches Zusammenwirken von Baukultur und Bauwirtschaft.

FINANCIAL AND CONCEPTUAL SUPPORT

Special thanks to our sponsors and institutions whose financial support has helped us so much with the production of this series of books. Their cultural commitment is a valuable contribution to fruitful and cordial collaboration between the culture and economics of architecture.

prohelvetia

JUNG

ALBRECHT JUNG GMBH & CO. KG, Schalksmühle

CONSFUTUR SINCE 1970

Consfutur, Mallorca

dade design concrete works

Dade Design AG, Altstätten

LÜCHINGER + MEYER

Dr. Lüchinger+Meyer Bauingenieure AG, Zürich

gae Gartenmann Engineering

Gartenmann Engineering AG, Zürich

GYSIN AG DESIGN. PRINT & COPYSHOP

GYSIN AG, Zürich

HUBER Fenster

Huber Fenster AG, Herisau

Schenker Storen

Schenker Storen AG, Zürich

SKY-FRAME

Sky-Frame AG, Frauenfeld

Isabel & Balz Baechi Foundation to protect wallpaintings, Zollikon

Tina Wüstemann, Partnerin Bär & Karrer AG, Zürich

Gus Wüstemann
104. Band der Reihe *De aedibus*
Herausgegeben von: Heinz Wirz, Luzern
Konzept: Heinz Wirz; gus wüstemann architects, Zürich
Projektleitung: Quart Verlag, Linus Wirz
Objekttexte: gus wüstemann architects
Textlektorat deutsch: Miriam Seifert-Waibel, Hamburg
Textlektorat englisch: Benjamin Liebelt, Berlin
Fotos: Walter Pfeiffer, Zürich S. 7; Bruno Helbling, Zürich S. 9–13, 16–17, 41–45, 49–51; gus wüstemann architects, Zürich S. 15, 23, 72–73; Zaborowsky Modellbauer, Zürich S. 57
Visualisierungen: Andrea Buchmeier, Zürich S. 19–21, 24–25; gus wüstemann architects, Zürich S. 27–29, 31–33, 36–37, 53–55, 7–69, 71; PLAY-TIME, Barcelona S. 35; Filippo Bolognese Images, Mailand S. 58–61; Zumo, Barcelona S. 63–65
Redesign: BKVK, Basel – Beat Keusch, Angelina Köpplin-Stützle
Grafische Umsetzung: Quart Verlag Luzern
Lithos: Rica Egger, Printeria, Luzern
Druck: DZA Druckerei zu Altenburg GmbH

Der Quart Verlag wird vom Bundesamt für Kultur für die Jahre 2021–2024 unterstützt.

ISBN 978-3-03761-264-4

Gus Wüstemann
Volume 104 of the series *De aedibus*
Edited by: Heinz Wirz, Lucerne
Concept: Heinz Wirz; gus wüstemann architects, Zurich
Project management: Quart Verlag, Linus Wirz
Project descriptions: gus wüstemann architects
German text editing: Miriam Seifert-Waibel, Hamburg
English text editing: Benjamin Liebelt, Berlin
Photos: Walter Pfeiffer, Zurich p. 7; Bruno Helbling, Zurich p. 9–13, 16–17, 41–45, 49–51; gus wüstemann architects, Zurich p. 15, 23, 72–73; Zaborowsky Modellbauer, Zurich p. 57
Visualisations: Andrea Buchmeier, Zurich p. 19–21, 24–25; gus wüstemann architects, Zurich p. 27–29, 31–33, 36–37, 53–55, 7–69, 71; PLAY-TIME, Barcelona p. 35; Filippo Bolognese Images, Milan p. 58–61; Zumo, Barcelona p. 63–65
Redesign: BKVK, Basel – Beat Keusch, Angelina Köpplin-Stützle
Graphic design: Quart Verlag Lucerne
Lithos: Rica Egger, Printeria, Lucerne
Printing: DZA Druckerei zu Altenburg GmbH

Quart Publishers is being supported by the Federal Office of Culture for the years 2021–2024.

ISBN 978-3-03761-264-4

Quart Verlag GmbH
Denkmalstrasse 2, CH-6006 Luzern
books@quart.ch, www.quart.ch

De aedibus
Zeitgenössische Architekturschaffende und ihre Bauten

De aedibus
Contemporary architects and their buildings

104 Gus Wüstemann (de/en)
103 frey architectes (de/en)
102 Masswerk Architekten (de/en)
101 Giorgis Rodriguez (de/en, es/fr)
100 Carlos Martinez (de/en)
99 Stocker Lee (de/en, it)
98 Roman Hutter (de/en)
97 Bachelard Wagner (de/en, fr)
96 Alain Wolff architectes (de/en, fr)
95 Horisberger Wagen (de/en)
94 Pont12 (de/en, fr)
93 Christian Dupraz (de/en, fr)
92 group8 (de/en, fr/en)
91 MPH (de/en, fr/en)
90 Spillmann Echsle (de/en)
89 Andy Senn (de/en)
88 Architetti Tibiletti Associati (de/en)
87 Zach + Zünd (de/en)
86 Kistler Vogt (de/en)
85 Sylla Widmann (de/en, fr/en)
84 Aebi & Vincent Architekten (de/en)
83 Baumberger & Stegmeier (de/en)
82 L-architectes (de/en, de/fr)
81 Frei Rezakhanlou (de/en)
80 weberbrunner (de/en)
79 Meyer Piattini (de/en)
78 meier + associés architectes (de/en, de/fr)
77 Lin Robbe Seiler (de/en, de/fr)
76 Meier Leder (de/en)
75 Butikofer de Oliveira Vernay (de/en)
74 Elisabeth & Martin Boesch (de/en)
73 spaceshop Architekten (de/en)
72 Kast Kaeppeli (de/en)
71 Philippe Meyer (de/en, fr)
70 bartbuchhofer (de/en)
69 Hauenstein La Roche Schedler (de/en)
68 Graeme Mann & Patricia Capua Mann (de/en)
67 Esposito Javet (de/en, de/fr)
66 Galletti Matter (de/en, de/fr)
65 Fruehauf, Henry & Viladoms (de/en)
64 Jakob Steib (de/en)
63 bunq (de/en)
62 Jean-Paul Jaccaud (de/en, de/fr)
61 huggenbergerfries (de/en)
60 Berrel Berrel Kräutler (de/en)
59 Pierre-Alain Dupraz (de/en, de/fr)
58 Cometti Truffer (de/en)
57 Joos & Mathys (de/en)
56 Lacroix Chessex (de/en)
55 Savioz Fabrizzi (de/en, de/fr)
54 Boegli Kramp (de/en)
53 Zita Cotti (de/en)
52 Oestreich + Schmid (de/en)
51 Stump & Schibli Architekten (de/en)
50 Luca Gazzaniga (de/en)
49 Guignard & Saner (de/en)
48 Morger + Dettli (de/en)
47 Charles Pictet (de/en)
46 Armando Ruinelli + Partner (de/en/it)
45 Luca Selva Architekten (de/en)
44 Luca Deon (de/en)
43 2b (de/en)
42 Durisch + Nolli (de/en)
41 sabarchitekten (de/en)
40 Beat Rothen (de/en)
39 Atelier Bonnet (de/en)
38 Novaron (de/en)
37 Althammer Hochuli (de/en)
36 Schneider & Schneider (de/en)
35 Frei & Ehrensperger (de, en)
34 Liechti Graf Zumsteg (de/en)
33 Adrian Streich (de/en)
32 Daniele Marques (de/en)
31 Neff Neumann (de/en)
30 Giraudi Wettstein (de/en)
29 Steinmann & Schmid (de/en)
28 Matthias Ackermann (de/en)
27 Aeby & Perneger (de/en)
26 Bakker & Blanc (de/en)
25 Markus Wespi Jérôme de Meuron (de/en)
24 Bauart (de/en, de/fr)
23 Knapkiewicz & Fickert (de/en)
22 Marcel Ferrier (de/en)
21 Wild Bär Architekten (de/en)
20 Enzmann + Fischer (de/en)
19 Mierta und Kurt Lazzarini (de/en)
18 Rolf Mühlethaler (de/en)
17 Pablo Horváth (de/en)
16 Brauen + Wälchli (de/en)
15 E2A Eckert Eckert Architekten (de/en)
14 Lussi + Halter (de/en)
13 Philipp Brühwiler (de/en)
12 Scheitlin – Syfrig + Partner (de/en)
11 Vittorio Magnago Lampugnani (de/en)
10 Bonnard Woeffray (de/en, de/fr)
9 Graber Pulver (de/en)
8 Burkhalter Sumi / Makiol Wiederkehr (de/en)
7 Gigon/Guyer (de, en)
6 Andrea Bassi (de, fr, en)
5 Dieter Jüngling und Andreas Hagmann (de, en)
4 Beat Consoni (de, en)
3 Max Bosshard & Christoph Luchsinger (de)
2 Miroslav Šik (de, en, it)
1 Valentin Bearth & Andrea Deplazes (de, en, it)

books@quart.ch, www.quart.ch